THE TRP TRICK

THE TRP TRICK

How Television in India was Hijacked

N Bhaskara Rao

Vitasta

LET KNOWLEDGE SPREAD

Published by
Renu Kaul Verma
Vitasta Publishing Pvt Ltd
2/15, Ansari Road, Daryaganj
New Delhi - 110 002
info@vitastapublishing.com

ISBN 978-93-86473-41-7

First Edition 2019
MRP ₹695

Editor: Papri Sri Raman
Cover and layout by Somesh Kumar Mishra
Printed by Vikas Computer and Printers

Dedicated to

Our grandchildren Udayaditya Palety, Isha and Diya Medasani.

Such a pleasure to engage and get into an argument with them, I get insights too. For, they are much smarter all round.

Contents

Foreword—I

Television in India, which began with experimental telecasts in 1956, has had a very interesting journey. It began with a focus on education and for many years continued to concentrate on education, in a broad sense of the term. Agriculture-linked programmes gained in prominence with the launch of Krishi Darshan in 1967. This was a prelude to the development-focussed Satellite Instructional TV Experiment (described by renowned sci-fi author Arthur Clarke as 'the greatest communication experiment' ever), which took television programmes to remote villages across 6 States in the country in 1975-76. In the decade and a half that followed, TV content was substantially related to development and social issues, though the end of the '80s saw the emergence of mythological programmes as a very popular genre, drawing huge audiences. Through this period, television was a monopoly of the state-run organisation, Doordarshan.

The 1990s saw a radical shift: competition to DD came in the form of first a few and then a spate of private foreign channels, all originating abroad and reaching the Indian viewer via satellite and cable, from uplink stations outside the country.

These channels brought in entertainment programmes in a massive way, all made with a great deal of sophistication, well-packaged and aggressively marketed. Given the very fragmented nature of the cable industry in India at the time, these channels could count on only small amounts of subscription revenue (from viewers), and had to adopt an advertising-based business model. After all, almost all were channels owned by private companies, here to tap India's potentially huge market to make a profit.

It is worth noting that these private channels—mostly foreign, but Indian ones too slowly beginning to emerge–definitely brought a breath of fresh air to an audience long-hungering for escapist entertainment (of the commercial feature film type) and well-packaged programmes. Television began to be seen as a source of low-cost entertainment for the family, far cheaper than going to a cinema theatre or any other outing. Little wonder, then, that satellite-dishes and cable connections sprouted even in poor neighbourhoods and slums across the country, as also in rural areas. Doordarshan yet continued to have a large—though declining—audience share (partly due to the many homes that yet could not afford a cable or DTH connection).

These developments brought about a sea-change in one major aspect of television. It was increasingly seen as a medium that delivered consumers to advertisers, rather than as one that provided meaningful content to citizens. Once the audience was perceived through this lens, the main interest of advertisers was clearly in reaching people who could consume their products—primarily the urban middle-class-plus viewers. Other viewers were of little interest to them. This meant that channels–which were dependent on advertisers for revenue—ensured that their programme content was such that it would appeal to the audience of interest to the advertiser. As both, audience and advertising grew, it became necessary for advertisers to make a proper assessment to decide which channel and what programmes to place their ads in. It is at this point that market research in the form of TRPs, Target Rating Points, entered the picture, as a way of helping advertisers by indicating the viewership and popularity of a programme.

In just a short while, TRPs practically became the be-all and end-all of programmes. Even DD, which—as an ostensible public-broadcaster—should have known better, succumbed and began looking at TRPs rather than the relevance or impact of its programmes. As is recognised, especially in the corporate world, metrics drives behaviour. TRP being the only metric that was (and continues to be) easily and regularly available, began to influence the 'behaviour' of all channels, DD included.

It is in this context of the growing importance of TRPs that this book is of such special relevance and significance. Understanding the background of Indian television, the origins of TV ratings, the work of various key organisations involved: all these are pertinent to the endeavour of comprehending the phenomenal hold of TRP on the TV landscape. And who better than Dr Bhaskara Rao to lead us through this? Dr Rao is a legendary figure and a pioneer in TV research in the country. He brings not only his professional expertise to bear on the issue, but provides deep insights because of his personal involvement in key developments of television in India. Having worked both within and outside the government, his inside knowledge combined with the objectivity of an independent researcher provides him—and, vicariously, the reader—a unique vantage point.

For anyone interested in understanding how ratings and TRPs have distorted the intent and purpose of TV in India, even as you take a journey through the history of TV, this is the book to read.

—Kiran Karnik
September 2018

Kiran Karnik was deeply involved with Krishi Darshan and SITE, and later developments in the television scene in India (including the Kheda/Pij project on local TV) while in ISRO. Subsequently, he was the first Director of Consortium for Educational Communication, which ran UGC's Countrywide Classroom programmes on television. Following this, he was responsible (as CEO) for the launch of Discovery Channel and Animal Planet in India and South Asia. His last full-time job was as President, NASSCOM, the association of India's IT industry.

Foreword II

Television ratings in India is the most controversial element of the media business in India since the unleashing of private channels and yet ratings continue to dictate and determine the content priorities of channels. In fact, the way TRP has become an yardstick of the industry is unprecedented and even intriguing. This book traces as never before and in a fascinating way, how it all happened unquestioned, using then- an-unknown meter and with a sample of a few hundred TV-owning households in Mumbai and Delhi to start with, and a few other cities much after a year. It is a surprise how no one before analysed this untold story on ratings and TRPs so tellingly!

Dr N Bhaskara Rao, who is known to different people differently, based on his contribution over the last five decades, is the one who had initiated media studies in India, including the first National Readership Study in the early seventies from ORG, Baroda, and studies on television when TV took off in India. It has been because of Dr Rao's extensive background from the very early years of television's growth that this book is able to describe the milestones in India's television and the twists and turns in that process in such an impartial way and as an independent researcher of distinct professional standing.

I agree with the contention of the book that creative genius, particularly storytelling and vocal culture of India being unique and generations old, television in India should have benefited far more in enriching itself with a distinct content model than ending up with the same old Western and consumer-centric content model. To facilitate the Western model of content delivery, as the book also explains, ratings were unleashed by the same elements of the industry as if in a *jugalbandhi* act. The book goes beyond and suggests ways of retrieving the television channels from the rating trap they are in.

Bhaskara Rao's book is a rare resource for channels, content producers and media planners. Even more for journalists, viewers and advertisers. They should read this book as it argues for win-win opportunities by taking to impact research than continuing with instant ratings. Academic departments of communication and media studies and those engaged in impact studies will benefit from this book. It offers insights for a new phase of Indian television to begin and correctives in research methodology.

The author reminds us of the irreversible impact of television, particularly on children and women and calls for preparedness and precautions.

The way television ratings are determined and used calls for urgent review and reposition, the book suggests. I think the way the television channels function requires such a review as a regular practice. I am glad the Ministry of Information & Broadcasting has now (since 16 April 2018) been seized of how viewership data has been somewhat vitiated, and this book corroborates this tweaking.

Based on extensive analysis of data hitherto not available to public, Rao points out that higher TRPs have not bettered either the quality of programmes or their creativity and relevance, nor have they improved the viability of channels even during the high-handed years of high TRPs. Too much reliance on TRPs has deprived channels from availing the best of opportunities and challenges. I have been witness to this status quo over the last couple of decades and can aver Rao's summation to be true. Reading this book will be an enriching experience even for viewers. This book is more than a reference source. It has insights for a reposition on the growth of television in India.

—Alok Mehta
Padma Shri
Senior Editor, Former President,
Editors Guild of India
New Delhi, September 2018

Preface

Television in India is 50 years old. But 'India specific TV' has not yet evolved and is not in sight, given the kind of grip the western 'content model' that channels have opted for in the last twenty-five years has over channels. In this quarter of a century, privatisation and competitive satellite channels have proliferated in this country as nowhere else in the world. Although a 'public service model' is rooted in Indian ethos and public communication culture, this could not sustain television channels in India as a TRP-driven model had perpetuated certain alien notions. All this happened simultaneously, as if rating agencies and foreign satellite channels were at tandem for a common mission of boosting consumerism and dominating the markets. There can be no doubt that in India, TRPs have favoured private satellite channels and even promoted a western content model.

The double-edged effects of television are well known. But what is not so much realised is that the ones with negative drive have higher potential and even get adopted under some kind of a constant duress. For, negative ideas and visual footage are far more appealing to the viewers to the extent of prompting greater bandwagoning and copycatting.

Content discrimination begins at a very young age. It is, therefore, at a very young viewer age that the ability to select positive content develops. Unless exposure to television is accompanied by parental care or societal counselling and becomes a concern of schools, a positive and proactive Indian television has no chance to emerge.

Negative effects of television are not because we are unconcerned and not because we do not have creative producers, but because television in India has lost its direction despite its potential to unleash a positive climate. This has happened because of the kind of rat-race that television channels were roped into for reasons external to viewers. A meter-based quantification, known to us as television rating points (or TRP), commercially driven (by revenue providing advertisers), has pre-emptied a pro-active model of television appropriate to basic needs and concerns of the people of the country.

As a staunch supporter of television for India, I have always maintained that television channels could accomplish for India in a decade what successive governments could not in more than six decades, if only the channels had been interested in determine strategies.

I still believe in such a potential for the visual media. It was with such a perspective that I looked at the growth and concerns of television channels in India over the decades. That was also the hope and expectations of India's visionaries. Based on almost fifty years of my pursuit of television in various capacities, I have identified TRP, the target rating, as a major disaster that Indian television has got bogged down in and there is no way in the immediate future to get out of the TRP's clutches in order to unleash the true potential of television in accomplishing the dreams of the people of India.

Most of the conclusions I have drawn in this book are based both, on my own personal experience of the medium and involvement directly or indirectly with its many and varied organisations and institutional functions. A retrospective view of what I apprehended 25-30 years ago about channels is what we are seeing playing out today. My personal involvement was at ORG (the Baroda-based Operations Research Group) first, followed by responsibilities at three Union ministries, and then initiatives from the Centre for Media Studies, including roundtable deliberations with rating agencies and countrywide discussions, formally and informally on content priorities.

The TRP or the quantitative survey for media goes back to the National Readership Survey of 1972, when in India, the major media was still the newspapers.

The report of first National Readership Survey (NRS) in India, conducted by ORG, came out in 1972-73 after one year of deliberations with stakeholders about the findings and their presentation protocol. Earlier, finalisation of the study design took one year for the consultation process with the three sponsors AAA (the Advertising Agencies' Associations), ISA (the Indian Society of Advertisers) and representatives of newspapers.

The concept of readership, listenership and viewership as well as the cut-offs for considering that and the format for presentation of reports were all decided in those deliberations. That was how the 'readership' idea gained ground in India and remained a credible yardstick over the years. The credibility of 'viewership' as a measure also is rooted in the same deliberations.

Even after all that process, as the one in charge at ORG, I faced court cases in 1973-74, in Rajasthan and Maharashtra.

The complaints were filed by two older publications as the ORG report indicated that newer dailies had higher readership. On that occasion, I went out of the way to explain how it could have happened, with detailed backup on spread of circulation of the dailies in context and with how one copy was read by a number of people over a 24-hour period (in the case of a daily).

Despite insights from conducting NRS two decades earlier, there are still no indications that TAM, the media research organisation of AC Nielsen and the Indian Market Research Bureau that did television viewership surveys, had gone through any such formal consultation process with stakeholders in India before pushing TRP as a bench-mark.

The subsequent NRS rounds and later, the Indian Readership Surveys (IRS), were measured by circulation of copies of newspapers that publications relied on. A pilot report for one State was brought out first (for Maharashtra), before releasing a national one which included all States and rural and urban areas. When IMRB described the second NRS (1975-76) which it did as 'national', although it covered only the urban reader, I protested in *Viduara*, the Press Institute of India's magazine almost twenty years later!

It was TAM/INTAM who promoted TRPs as 'national' although they covered hardly ten cities in India in the first couple of years. There are 4,000 cities and towns in India. About 300 cities have population over 100,000 each. Seven cities have population of more than 3 million. So, when Television Advertisement Measurement Private Limited calls a survey 'national', it must be of smples of at least a thousand towns, including half the number from rural India.

Guidelines of the Telecom Regulatory Authority of India

should have meant a rethink on the methodology framework and the way the viewership ratings continue to be relied on by channels. But then, why has that not happened?

BARC, the Broadcast Audience Research Council of India, took five years to come into play despite backup from TRAI, the Telecom Regulatory Authority of India, the Information and Broadcasting Ministry and key stakeholders. If its methodology is the same (or almost same) and its concern is limited to weekly viewer ratings as before, without considering impact and implications, what difference can it be expected to make? In any case, if the agency which unleashed TRP regime in India in the previous twenty years continues to be a player in a new avatar, can we expect much-needed shifts in the paradigm of ratings?

Without civil society's concerns about the way the role of television is looked upon and transparency is ensured all across, can we expect any repositioning of television in India so that an 'Indian television' gets revitalised.

For the last one decade, the independent body, Centre for Media Studies has been doggedly questioning the very basis of the TRP approach that is accepted unquestioningly by television channels to select content and the relevance of such an accounting.

My pursuit of role, credibility and potential of media spans over more than three decades. Professor GNS Raghavan and I argued in 1996 about the Social Effects of Media. Why we should be concerned about the 'social effect' of television and more recently (in 2012), I also had occasion to describe why and how news channels in India have not been able to 'unleash their potential' (2013). In between, there were several other research studies that I was involved in. This book benefits from insights from these studies.

The Reuters Institute's 2017 Digital News Project (Nic Newman and Richard Fletcher), in their report, *Bias, Bullshit and Lies-Audience Perspectives on Low Trust in Their Media,* reminds us of what CMS had indicated two decade ago, *reasons for low trust in the news channels* because of bias, spin and agendas. And that is because 'powerful people are using the media to push their own political or economic interests'. (https://reutersinstitute.politics.ox.ac.uk/)

This book is relevant because even after change in the agency offering viewership rates, the architecture of the meter and the methodology followed by BARC for viewership is by and large the same. This book offers insights into correctives at different levels and by different stakeholders.

It is important that BARC succeeds in restoring credibility and rejuvenates the creative potential of India's genius for an Indian television that can occupy a pride of place globally. This should be the concern of the Ministry of Information and Broadcasting which has now (in 2018) revived the idea of built-in chips in television set top boxes, for presumably 'more reliable viewership data'. Since the concern of the book is TRPs, the analysis in this book is focussed on its prime years in the '80s-'90s and the first decade of the new century. A close analyses for 2014-2020 period may reveal a more fascinating perspective of the television scenario in India.

I thank Kiran Karnik, doyen of development communication and Alok Mehta, senior editor, for their extensive forewords to this work. I thank Renu Kaul Verma of Vitasta Publishing and editor Papri Sri Raman for her thorough editing of the book.

The Past and the Present of Indian Television

WE KNOW how more than two hundred years ago the British had won India. But do we know or have we ever realised that thirty years ago, television ratings too gripped the minds of the people of India with a similar 'wizard' model? We know who or what East India Company was all about. But we do not know even now fully the true origins of the TRPs that television follows in India. From a general research tool encompassing quality, quantity and several other parameters and called Target Rating Point, how did it metamorph into a quantitative television viewership rating for India specifically? Despite marked difference, this quantity-based TRP has made it to the country's mind-set and sets programme scheduling priorities for channels. Interestingly, successive governments did nothing and by the time they realised its mind space-controlling potential, it was thought to be too late politically to take corrective initiatives. If with just 500 meters read (survey respondents), India could be put on a TRP-set course believed to be 'irreversible', is it not a never-before perpetrated hoax on the people of India?

Even more astonishing is the fact that in a country of active citizenry, academic faculties and as many creative minds including in the media of the country, no one questioned the basics and logics of an inane methodology on which TRPs continued to rely on for three decades and determined the kind of television India has ended up with! By the time authorities woke up to the danger of such a limited assessment, the TRPs' hold on the channels was suffocating, these numbers controlled a channel's every breath and all channels telecasting in India felt deprived of their oxygen without such a deceptive support. So also, the advertising businesses. It became a *jugalbandhi* hard to break![1]

Not much has been written to explain the compulsions of television in India to rely on a TRP system to judge society's need, despite the fact that there is so much to unravel and aspire to.

The TRP-driven model has deprived Indian television from becoming the tool for dramatic socio-economic change, given its wide reach (total daily tune-ins on TV is 566+ million according to a BARC report in 2017). Can we ever retrieve the situation to realise the kind of potential television has in India? There is no public explanation of the kind of path and processes India has gone through in adopting its particular content model. In this book, I attempt to unravel what I call the 'TRP trap'[2] and how television in India has been hijacked to serve some interests. *How, why and in whose interest? Has that model made channels any relevant and India-specific?* These are some of my questions.

It took India twenty years (1992-2012) to wake up to TRP, a scam threatening the very basic characteristics of Indian society and depriving television the creative potential of its people. It took another five years for the successive governments to initiate corrective measures. What was it that made the country behave like a banana republic in this context?

One must remember India holds top position globally both with respect to ICT (Information Communication Technologies) and applications software, it is the country which was first in 1975 to launch SITE (Satellite Instructional Television Experiment). In 1991-93, the same country submitted to a regime by a foreign-controlled company, using less than 500 viewership meters brought from Canada and Africa, that offered *television viewership ratings* for the entire country (TRP). Of course, once the woolly idea of TRPs was established, mysteriously, in no time, these meters were replaced in Mumbai and Delhi where they had been installed with the ubiquitous 'people meter'. This would not have been possible without advertisers and advertising agencies coming together to promote and perpetuate that arrangement and system in tandem with their budgets and businesses.

A conspiracy theory has been that TRP was a ploy of the global consumer lobby. It opened the floodgates to the huge Indian markets without them having to go through any negotiations, like at the WTO. Once the 'Indian market' was open, after the economic liberalisation of 1991, all that market manipulators had to do was e-capture the existing consumer markets in the quickest possible way. Just as trade and commerce was the East India Company's way of capturing India, TRP was an instrument for capturing the markets and minds of the people of India, particularly those with deep pockets. This could not have been possible without promoting the priorities by the mass media. And television, by the 1990s, was well on its way to becoming India's cheapest mass media.

The understanding of global commercial interests was, if Indian values, family system, societal standing of women, creative faculties of children and life styles are destabilised, what would be left that is Indian and unique to its culture and living styles? Nothing. Nothing uniquely Indian. Therefore, can India be changed? Can India be reduced to being viewed as a mass market for consumer products? In twenty years, this is what TRPs have done, taking advantage of television's potential in India.

To cultivate a mass market requires homogenised minds and harmonised markets. In the '90s, that was possible only through television. No other single instrument had such a simultaneous reach and penetrating power. Mass media paves the way for capturing the economic markets and opens wide the minds and lures the country into newer consumption options and promotes consumerism, replacing a 'culture of conservation' which is based on preserving natural resources for the future and sustaining civilisation. Global commerce possibly wanted to destroy India's 'culture of conservation' and promote mass consumerism in India, given India's numbers. Its one billion people. In a nutshell, this is what the conspiracy allegation about TRP and content priorities of TRP-driven television implies.

This also enables dominance of mass media, particularly that dependent on technology that needs high investment. Television has always been technology driven, both for entertainment and news channels. The innocuous TRP booby targeted three birds in one go—domination of markets, mass media and the minds of the masses of the country. Doesn't it sound too good for coincidence?

If Aadhar and Facebook can be accused for data collection and misuse of it, with or without knowledge and concurrence of individuals, how come the TRP data process and practice never came under the scanner, even when instances of manipulation had been reported in the media and complaints were made by competing media to the government?

Going by what the Facebook promoter, Mark Zuckerberg, had admitted (9 April 2018) to the US Congress in the course of testimony and his own public apology for misuse of data, irrespective of his awareness both for what its business model was and reliability of its methodology was, TRP in India should have also gone through a minimum public scrutiny two decades ago. No one ever asked how a meter (both, the imported ones and the so-called people meter) was recording and how its reading was interpreted and projected to the nation.

What Motivated India to Go for Television?

Unlike in the USA, television was not invented in India. It came to India not as a result of market forces, not even due to global entrepreneurs, nor as a result of foreign investments. The technology had been there since 1927, a gift to the world by a 21-year-old technology buff. Its use was popularised during World War II, to show the world this worldwide conflict. After the war ended, nations used the technology according to their needs. Television in India was the result of an outlook of its visionaries.

It was India's first Prime Minister, Jawaharlal Nehru's enthusiasm for scientific temper in people and fascination for modern technology for India that created interest in television as an 'instrument for development'.

Thus, television arrived in India in 1959, as part of a national development agenda of the government. The vision was altruistic.[3]

By then, television had made inroads into the lives of the ordinary people of Europe and the USA. The *Sesame Street* serial (Ford Foundation supported), for example, was a much-acclaimed children's television programme by then.

The oral historian Douglas Ensminger, a proactive Representative of Ford Foundation in India (1967-70), quickly took up the idea with Indira Gandhi soon after she became the Prime Minister. Instead of waiting for a full channel, it was decided to take up television telecasting on an experimental basis by the All India Radio as a part of its programmes for farmers and rural communities. The *Krishi Darshan* serial (weekly thrice for 30 minutes) was the first Indian production for television. It was telecast as an integral part of the then-piloted Green Revolution or intensive agriculture extension programme, which was by then a national mission. It was then that Doordarshan, as India's first television broadcaster, was born in the Broadcast House of All India Radio, with focus on farmers, children and families. In 1972, India's second television station was opened in Bombay, followed by stations in Amritsar and Srinagar (in 1973) and Madras, Calcutta and Lucknow (in 1975).

The scientist, Vikram Sarabhai, much before his becoming the Chairman of Indian Space Research Organisation, espoused the potential of television for India's development and growth path. His idea was pursued almost a decade later (1975-77) with SITE (Satellite Instruction Television Experiment). Here television technology was married with satellite transmission in India. It was the first ever experiment to use satellites for development of broadcasting to specified grassroots communities in multiple languages simultaneously.

The focus continued to be on agriculture and education. Health, rural development and family planning were later added. Entertainment was not a focus. A basic understanding was that television is the best bet for awareness, attitude creation, knowledge dissemination, to steer behavioural change and for promoting good practices. Television was viewed as a better medium for social change, economic development and a reliable instrument for people to adopt sustainable life styles and become a stakeholder in governance.

A very interested Indira Gandhi named the broadcaster Doordarshan, she also suggested the first tag line, 'Satyam Shivam Sundaram'—signifying information, education and empowering endeavours. PV Krishna Murthy was the first Director General of Doordarshan, which functioned as a media unit of the Ministry of Information & Broadcasting.

To begin with, India had adopted television with an objective that it will strengthen national integration, enrich its cultural roots, support education, deepen democracy, spread knowledge, facilitate equity in socio-economic development, provide news and current affairs and also empower people at large. Any appraisal of television in India 50 years later cannot be begun with any other yardsticks. Although at the outset, television was piloted with programmes to facilitate 'lab to land' transmission—as an agriculture extension service to facilitate rural uplift—it was soon extended in support of education and literacy.

India took to colour television in 1982 after much deliberation, hoping that it will motivate people to become nature lovers, sensitive to issues and that it would appeal to people to take to newer lifestyles with a 'modern/civilised outlook'. However, with quick proliferation of channels, and most expansion being outside Doordarshan and in a competitive way, the scope and priorities of content changed in a matter of two decades.

An analysis of contents of main television channels in English, Hindi and Telugu sums up the kind of concerns that television was preoccupied with in its first two decades. The analysis, presented for a recent decade, is self-explanatory and brings out in no uncertain terms that television in India has pursued altogether a different course and agenda than what was envisioned in the early years. How did it all happen? When did such a reversal in the priorities of television start? What prompted such a focus shift? It did not happen overnight. But that has not been seriously looked into with critical analysis or as to what difference the content concerns have made.

Who decides the contents of television? People, viewers, government, channels themselves, investors into channels, or advertisers or is it TRPs! Whoever it may be, there should be a logic. People are likely to benefit from television and expect to get some useful support service. Viewers like to get entertained too. And learn or come to know something or the other of their interest or all these aspects in a certain combination.

Channels obviously like to see that they are most viewed; investors for sure want to get more and more return for their investment in the channel and profit; advertisers like to see that services, products and brands they sponsor, or support are sold and acquire mass market and loyalty too. Best thing about television is that in India, telecast serves or caters to multiple interests parallelly. Channels can do so, provided they can balance so many interests. Can they? An analysis of contents brings out a different picture.

In my book, *Unleashing Power of News Channels*[4] (EMESCO, 2012 & Adroit, 2017), I indicated that even after twelve years of presence in India, news channels have not realised their potential fully. They did not even increase viewership, proportionate to increase in the number of news channels.

My earlier book, *Poll Surveys in Media – An Indian Perspective*[5] (National Book Trust, 2012), brought out that news channels did not make much difference in the election process, neither in terms of enlightening viewers in making better voting choices, nor have they benefitted the poll process in any way. For example, the 'Note-for-vote phenomena' has increased after proliferation of television and the voter turnout has not increased much. In fact, there have been instances of decline in turnout where exposure to news television is more. News television is often accused of trivialising poll campaigns and competition between parties and candidates. Nevertheless, news channels continue to be engaged in claiming higher and higher viewership, not in making a difference in the electoral process for the better.

More than half of the 800+ television channels in the country are round-the-clock news channels. And yet, what has been the viewership? It is the entertainment content in all channels including in the news channels, which have increased.

In the last four years (2014-18), more news channels have been specifically credited with sensitising the larger public

Table 1: Number of TV Channels by Genre

Category of Channels	2000*	2010#	2016#
News	7	258	399
Entertainment	100	145	290
Sports	5	8	35
Spiritual	2	17	53

Sources*:Television Channels in India: Strategic Growth Perspectives (the Year 2000 data belongs to this source). FICCI + KPMG Report 20166 (Year 2000 data belongs to this source also).
Source#: Master List of Permitted Private Satellite TV Channel by I&B Ministry till 31-12-2016.

Table 2: Viewership of Different Genre Channels 2015

Total viewership 886 million			
	Reach of total population	% Share in total viewers	
News	57,500,000	Hindi News 3.0% Regional News 3.5% English News 0.0%	Total 6.5%
Entertainment	742,400,000	Regional GEC 29.6% Hindi GEC 28.4% Hindi Movies 13.4% Regional Movies 6.6% Regional Music 2.7% Music 2.6% English Entertainment -0.5%	Total 83.8%
Sports	18,600,000	2.1%	
Spiritual	7,974,000	0.9%	

Source: - FICCI + KPMG Report 2016.[6]

Table 3: Trends in Contents of News Bulletins 2005-2016
Reversal of the Trend with Proliferation of News Channels

	2005	2006	2007	2008	2009*	2010	2011	2012	2013	2014*	2015	2016
Politics	23.10	11.80	11.24	10.49	20.36	12.47	17.68	28.69	28.63	43.03	33.36	23.13
Sportsww	10.70	19.20	16.99	20.97	16.03	17.93	16.09	13.06	10.04	5.96	5.74	2.69
Crime	9.40	10.50	11.06	4.61	4.86	5.74	5.16	6.63	8.31	3.92	5.01	5.06
Entertainment	6.10	11.50	15.97	13.44	10.13	12.74	9.72	10.16	9.58	7.08	5.66	5.01
Agriculture	0.10	0.50	0.19	0.29	0.18	0.19	0.09	0.08	0.05	0.18	0.65	0.14
Education	1.10	0.90	0.69	0.66	0.85	0.51	0.60	0.63	0.69	1.48	0.50	1.30
Health	1.20	2.20	0.85	1.01	1.87	1.19	1.00	1.00	1.06	1.20	2.97	1.28
Environment	0.40	0.50	0.88	0.77	1.53	1.29	0.84	0.66	0.32	0.76	1.76	1.57

Source: CMS Media Lab[7]

*Year 2009 and Year 2014 were general election years.

about corruption in the country and even exposing many of the corruption scams. But there are some who accuse television news channels of diffusing issues and distracting attention from issues that matter really.[8] Political news transmission and viewing was high in the election years 2009 and 2014, as the data show. Therefore, news channels dished out more of political news than any other kind of news. Everything else took a backseat, whether viewers liked it or not. Sports content had the next highest viewership in the earlier decades but data from 2015 show dominance of entertainment channels and viewership.

Entertainment channels, their serials particularly, are being criticised for depicting and portraying women in a vampish way and for eroding family values and dividing people more, spreading suspicion rather than helping in confidence-building among people. They lack the much-needed healing touch. At the same time no one will say that television today portrays reality or even grassroots reality among any section of society. There are, of course, a few exceptions but nationally and regionally, instances of exaggerated or unrealistic coverage are far more.

A rights regime has been adopted in the last decade but how much empowered are people today? The Right to Information remains intact as an Act because of civil society and the media, including news television channels. However, it is to be taken note of that the spread and proliferation of television in the country in the last two decades should have moved the rights regime forward. Has that happened?

Television viewers continue to be mostly women and children. As such, it is important that the country knows the impact of television contents on them or how television can work adversely. Contrary to general belief and theoretical propositions, atrocities and abuses against children and women in the country in the last decade have more than doubled and is steadily going up, as if there is a stimulus in the atmosphere. This was discussed in my book, *Unleashing the Power of News Channels*.

More than a decade ago my book with Professor GNS Raghavan, *Social Impact of Mass Media of India*[9] (1996 Gyan) brought out the kind of influence that television content meant. Time spent by children watching television is anywhere from one hour to four hours on holidays. Television has deprived children from outdoor physical activity. And this is just one observation.

Instead of scientific temper, television has promoted blind faith and belief. The data shows us that over the decade, not only has the number of channels in the genre of spiritualism and religion multiplied, but the overall thrust of television serials has been in this direction and it is viewership of such programming that has increased. Are we more irrational and impatient people today? Yes, we are. One of the hopes of supporting television's entry and growth in India was that it would promote a rational outlook and improve scientific temper in people in general and children in particular and make the average citizen more active. Has that happened? What has been the trend?

Sarabhai's Vision of a Television for India

Vikram Sarabhai can be described as one of the founders of modern India. A great visionary, Sarabhai put India on a game-changer course among the world's nations. It was his pioneering initiatives which took India on the growth path in multiple fields. These include satellite communication and growth of television. At the same time, the nation needs to ask itself, how come, despite Vikram Sarabhai's foresight and exemplary initiative to unleash the power of satellites for India's communication needs and development endeavours, India took an altogether different course? Did his sudden death in 1972 stop India from pursuing a India-specific model for India to become a unique global knowledge base? It was this thought that has led me to study the trajectory of television in today's India.

My meeting with Vikram Sarabhai[10] in 1971 at India International Centre, New Delhi, not only changed my career path but also the growth path of the Operations Research Group, a pioneer research outfit of that times. More specifically, that discussion with Sarabhai has helped me unleash media research in India and laid the path for independent and objective applied social and market research in the country, including media research. The visionary's parting advise to me was: 'Ford Foundation is not where you should be, you should go to ORG, Baroda…There is so much to do'. He inspired me to take applied social research to a national level and scale this up nationwide.

Sarabhai was in discussions at that time with NASA (the American space agency) for the first of its kind experiment to use satellites for broadcasting and to do so simultaneously in multiple languages, to cater to different regions of India. He believed that television was the best medium to overcome India's basic problems—that is literacy, health, agriculture, skills and citizenship. Instead of limiting satellite and television technologies to economic policies for poverty eradication in

India, he argued for using modern technology for national development. It was a coincidence that Indira Gandhi too initially believed so. She had been India's I&B Minister from 1964-to 1966. However, television remained in an experimental phase till about 1965.

The Kheda Communications Project was set up under SITE as a pilot project that would be replicated in rural India in 1974. The village selected for India's first local rural television telecast was the obscure hamlet of Pij in Kheda district of Gujarat. A low-powered transmitter gifted by United Nations Development Programme (UNDP) and a local production studio was set up at Pij while a satellite earth station was set up at Ahmedabad's Space Applications Center (SAC). Next, 651 televisions sets were distributed among the residents of 400 villages in a 35 km radius. Thus, on a sultry evening in July 1975, over 100 excited villagers huddled together at a ground in Pij, their eyes glued to the wooden box with a blank glass screen in front of them.

As a senior advisor about a decade later at the Ministry of I&B, I assisted the then Union Minister Vasant Sathe (1981-83) when certain (economic) departments of the government opposed colour television in India because of high investments that it involved (they cited the examples of Sri Lanka and Nepal). In a cabinet note, we successfully argued in favour of colour television. One other point we made in that note was that colour television motivates people better, it will support development plans and help scale up good practices and that environment protection will receive a boost. So, if we look back at contemporary history, even as recently as 1981, Sarabhai's idea of a 'entertainment-education model'[11] of television for

India received a push and gained ground. All this changed, however, in the mid-1990s with the opening up of the Indian economy.

Liberalisation allowed private sector entry in a competitive mode. In the years 1991 to 1998, 'television for national cause' was quietly forgotten. What should surprise us most is that no sane voice stood up to question the shift in the nation's policy priority.

Indian Institute of Mass Communication

Wilbur Schramm[12] was an early proponent of 'communication media for development'. He wrote extensively as a professor at Harvard, Stanford, MIT and Hawai East-West Centre. Prof Everett M Rogers,[13] another pioneer and proponent of 'Diffusion of Innovation', too advocated communication media for agriculture and family planning practices and for adopting better behavioural practices. Both of them advocated relevance and role of electronic media in that context for India, as against the model in vogue in the USA in the 1970s.

Schramm met Prime Minister Indira Gandhi and convinced her to start an institute to train people for using media for development. The birth of the Indian Institute of Mass Communication (IIMC) in New Delhi as a part of the Ministry of Information and Broadcasting was his recommendation. In that connection Laj Narain, an Information Service officer, even visited the USA (in 1967), to understand how to set up such an institution. I was one of the persons he had a discussion with at the University of Iowa in 1968. That IIMC lost its way in five or six years and has today become a journalism school with focus on a 'public relations approach' is another story.

I was requested in 1975 to head IIMC by the then I&B Minister, IK Gujral. I only agreed to be a Visiting Professor and set up the Research and Evaluation department and built these faculties at the IIMC during my tenure from 1974 to 1977. Professor Pradipto Roy, an associate of Everett Rogers, appraised the IIMC in 1973 and pointed out the need to build research (appraisal) capabilities and made out a case for a 'development paradigm' for the media, with television playing a key role in that process. All those early initiatives and insights faded with the entry of the TRP as an instrument of measuring and promoting consumerism.

Television as a Development Tool

Learnings from Krishi Darshan, Vikram Sarabhai's vision for India, Wilbur Schramm and Everett Rogers' advice, research-based insights from around the globe, the SITE experiment in particular and later, the Pij station in Gujarat's Kheda village—all of them had offered a model of telecast that India should adopt and absorb as a part of her national development endeavours. It was distinct from the models in vogue, particularly in the US (although its children's serial *Sesame Street*[14] series had a global reach). An example before television in India was the content model of All India Radio (AIR), with a mix of culture, entertainment, news and education that was well appreciated because of its participative and inclusion of people approach that the AIR had followed.

After Pij, in the early '80s, television sets for community viewing were set up in some of the most backward and remote villages of six States (Bihar, Orissa, Madhya Pradesh, Rajasthan, Andhra Pradesh and Karnataka), with programmes covering crucial subjects such as health, agriculture and education. In 1984, the Kheda Communications Project won the UNESCO Prize for rural communication efficiency. However, in 1985 (when Doordarshan set up its full-fledged facility at Ahmedabad) it was decided that the Pij transmitter would be moved to Chennai for a second channel. This decision was greeted by protests by the locals who were deeply attached to the historic transmitter and even started a 'Pij TV Kendra Bachao' movement. Nevertheless, the Pij tower went to Chennai.

Pune Film and Television Institute, FTVI

By the mid-70s, the Ministry also set up the short-lived prototype development centre at the Pune Film and TV Institute of India (FTVI) at the instance of Jim Beveridze, a well-known Canadian scholar. In the years 1974 to '77, he showcased how films can be used for development and how visual media can be used for educating the masses. At the FTVI, Bashiruddhin Ahmed of Osmania University and half a dozen researchers endeavoured to demonstrate how field research-supported content model could help television make a difference. Beveridze soon decided to leave India as he was unhappy as no television Kendra of the Doordarshan was adopting the research-based programming model that he had suggested.

In 1975, I had occasion to review the work of this Centre at the Pune Film & TV Institute, which the government decided to close down without waiting for my report, perhaps because its supporter in the Ministry, Jamal Kidwai, the Secretary, too had put in his papers in the wake of the declaration of National Emergency.

All these expert recommendations had urged India to adopt an India-specific content model for television. Even more important, India had another advantage, its epics, *Ramayana* and Mahabharata, children stories like *Panchatantra*, *Jataka Kathas* and many folk and oral narratives which could provide a ready and clear model and offer a basis and framework for the growth of specifically an 'Indian model of television programming' for people to quickly absorb the growth stories. I maintain that these would have made much more difference than *Tom and Jerry*, or *Micky Mouse* and other children's serials. As an 'entertainment-education' model, values and concerns would have been very different from what has evolved from a US-like model. The copycatting excluded creativity.

Three Aspects of Liberalisation

Three developments of the time much later preoccupied public attention. First, opening India to private television channels abruptly, without any debate, preparations and regulatory framework on any aspect of contents left the viewer rudderless, swimming in a plethora of content without the wherewithal to choose good from the bad. Secondly, all of a sudden, from a few hours of government-controlled transmission, the Indian viewer was exposed to a 24-hour programming format without channels having any clarity on content strategies and without guidelines. Thirdly, immediately also came up channels offering exclusive 24-hour news contents and bulletins. This flood of content and viewer time simply overwhelmed the Indian viewer, more than fifty per cent of who were women and children.

The *India Today* group first started news transmission on Doordarshan as a weekly programme called *News Track*[15] and once private channels were allowed, *India Today* launched its own channel. Doordarshan also transmitted *World This Week* with Prannoy Roy as the anchor. By then, he had come to be known as an election analyst on television. As an economist, he had ventured into election time analysis along with Ashok Lahiri (both from the Delhi School of Economics then) for the *India Today* magazine in early 1980s.

Advertisement Comes to Television

Sometime in 1972-73, Gerson daCunah of Lintas had suggested to I&B Secretary Jamal Kidwai to make the government's Directorate of Advertising and Visual Publicity, DAVP, into a public-private enterprise. His note detailed a model of operation which allowed government departments to go to private advertising agencies for their campaigns instead of limiting them to the DAVP. Kidwai saw some merit in the suggestion and had allowed some consultations between DAVP and private advertising agencies on creative aspects.

In 1976, there was a discussion and a committee set up in the Ministry of Information & Broadcasting on whether commercial advertising[16] should be allowed on Doordarshan. In a way, this was also a turning point which paved the way for a TRP-led programming. All India Radio's commercial centre in Bombay had brought a proposal from one of the companies (the then Richardson Hindustan, later a part of Proctor & Gamble) in Bombay with an offer of big money if allowed to advertise its personal grooming brands on Doordarshan.[17]

Until 1975, only a few Doordarshan Kendras inserted public service messages in between feature programmes. Minister VC Shukla discussed the proposal with the then Directors

General of Doordarshan and AIR, Shailendra Shankar and PC Chatterjee. Nandlal Chawla, who succeeded me at IIMC as a Visiting Professor and later as its Director, an old-timer at All India Radio and I were also present. Deputy Minister Dharma Bir Sinha and I opposed the idea of opening Doordarshan for commercials but Shukla was inclined to accept the Mumbai offer. The others present were also not affirmative about the proposal. The meeting ended with a suggestion that Chawla and I go to Bombay and discuss with leading advertising bosses and come up with a proposal. *There was absolutely no voice suggesting that the authorities consider viewer opinions on telecast of such commercials.* In a two-day visit to Bombay, Chawla and I discussed the possibilities in one-to-one meetings with some stalwarts of the time, including Gerson daCunah, RK Swamy, Roger Pereira of Shilpi, K Kurian of Radius, Chawla, Director, media planning of HTA, Sarma of Sistas, and others. We also met Guru Charan Das of Richardson Hindustan.

Chawla and I could not come up with an unanimous report. After discussing with Dharma Bir Sinha, I gave a report opposing brand advertising on Doordarhsan but suggested a 'sponsored' type of presentation. It could be presented like…'this programme is brought to you by Tata Sons, manufacturers of salt'…. It could be telecast as commercials between two feature programmes, without interrupting any feature programme.

Minister Shukla went along with the idea of a 'revenue maximisation model' (as in vogue in the USA) that Nandlal Chawla had presented. That was how television advertising in India has come to stay and dictate not just the content model but also the very growth of television in India and the viewership rating mechanism.

This transition happened much before a TRP era. But then, this opening up of Doordarshan for consumer and brand advertising facilitated a decade later a shift in the content priorities, once investments and entry into the Indian market were opened up for multinationals and their advance support services, including advertising and associated businesses.

A few years later, at ORG, when I was monitoring reports of advertisements in newspapers, All India Radio and Doordarshan, I realised that sometimes there was crowding of commercials at certain timings of certain (film-based) feature programmes. I also observed from field surveys in other contexts that there was a certain amount of resentment from viewers against such concentration of commercials in the middle of certain popular programmes.

When Indira Gandhi came back to power in 1980-03, she suggested to Vasant Sathe, the new Minister for I&B, to have a high-level Standing Advisory Committee for I&B policy issues. A former senior advisor to Jawaharlal Nehru and later to Indira Gandhi, G Parthasarathy was made to head that committee. It included a few eminent personalities like Narayan Menon, the first Indian Director General of AIR, Mulk Raj Anand, the author, Kartar Singh Duggal, Fathima Zakaria of *Times of India*, Alkazi of the National School of Drama and me.

In this committee, in a 1982 meeting, I brought up the issue of crowding of commercials on Doordarshan and suggested that not more than ten per cent of telecast time should be permitted for commercials. Also, that commercial should be spread across, across the broadcast duration, if they cannot be limited to in-between programmes. That was how the idea of a ceiling on ads has become a policy directive. But there was no evidence that this was ever implemented strictly, once a multiplying of channels started after 1990. In 2013, it was the sector regulator TRAI, that imposed a 12-minute cap based on CMS studies in the previous years, and made it an obligation on the part of channels to submit 'volume of advertisement time' on a quarterly basis.

50 Years of Indian TV

Television in India has completed fifty years. And yet, and despite efforts in the initial years, an 'Indian television' has not evolved. The model of television system that we have ended up with is alien to India. It is western in nature. It is advertising-determined and a 'more the merrier' model. A model for 'more viewers somehow, and by any means'.

It is not based on lessons or insights from our own experiences. Nor is it based on lessons from the American model of television, which has vast research base to draw upon. India has not tried to improve upon that US model or draw upon her own creative potential and wealth of heritage. Even coverage of basic issues, challenges before the country and socio-economic issues have not become the priorities of television contents.

Five Phases

Indian television has witnessed five distinct phases of about a decade each. To start with, India had adopted television with an objective that it will strengthen national integration, enrich its cultural roots, provide news and current affairs and offer scintillating entertainment and empower people at large. Nothing of that sort has happened in the last fifty years.

Phase I: The first phase of formative years (1970-80) was

of experiments—localised experiments to use television for rural communities and then for school broadcasts. This phase had witnessed two key policy initiatives. The first was with a programme prototype research centre at Pune Film Institute, followed by SITE, using satellite for simultaneous telecast in four different languages spread across 2,400 villages of six States over a period of one year. The content was purposely selected in support of development endeavours. A part of this experiment was the Pij community television station in Gujarat to demonstrate use of television for local needs and aspirations, with participation of locals.[18]

Another policy initiative was the launch of Prasar Bharati to develop public service broadcasting for India.

Phase II: The second phase of television in India (1980-90) was one of liberating television from the black and white era into a world of colours, and also from that of government clutches with a hope that it could reach out more and also motivate many more. By going colour and taking to soap opera serials, television in India had arrived on the global television space. By opening up India for private television, the Indian market was connected or plugged into a larger global market.

Well before the radical shift in the paradigm of media in India and before TRP took television by storm, there were a number of insights available to us from India's cultural traditions and cinema, and All India Radio. *And, there were no differences among political leaders of India about use of television for development and education instead of going for an entertainment orientation.*

A turning point was a discussion that Prime Minister Indira Gandhi had with the iconic Miguel Sabido of Mexico in

1983.[19] Sabido has been credited globally for a distinct model of television contents, with 'entertainment-education' approach-based serials as soap operas. It was after that meeting, that a team including the I&B Secretary SS Gill[20] went to Mexico for interaction with Sabido along with writer Manohar Joshi. The *Humlog* serial on Doordarshan (1984-85) was an immediate outcome of those parleys. Indian television thereafter took to serialisation of sitcoms or soap operas. Doordarshan followed that success with *Buniyad* (1986-87), *Ramayana* (1987-88), *Mahabharata* (1988-90) and many more serials. There was no indication at that time of any decline in the viewership of Doordarshan. About fifteen years later, these were some of the serials that Star TV repeated (or wanted to but could not), once TRP was made the yardstick for channels.

Phase III: The third phase (1990-2000) witnessed unprecedented proliferation of private television across the country, particularly in regional languages. And even more importantly, multiplying of channels—particularly the twenty-four hour news channels—all gearing up to new economic realities and direct-to-home broadcasting, DTH. This helped consolidate the content model that channels were opting for and settled on.

Phase IV: The fourth phase of Indian television (2000-2012) featured the rise and rise of TRPs swaying the market, rather driving television industry in India. This model imitated the west formally as if there could never be a reversal. It projected viewer quantity as the only way towards viability, which means luring more and more viewers and attracting foreign investments into competitive markets.

Phase V: The fifth has been (2013-2020) a phase of

realisation that TRPs cannot be relied upon too much at the cost of creative potential and also the rise of opinion in favour of regulatory restrains from within. There is also realisation that programming always has newer opportunities and content can be about the basic concerns of people even outside the 'consumer markets'.

However, there are no indications so far that television in India will any time soon reverse its direction and content priorities in a big way. The 'reality shows' have not helped much. This is perhaps because neither consolidation of channels, nor their viability has become any better. Mergers and acquisitions of television channels and entry of 'big industry' in that process has consolidated 'more of the same' and adopted the prevalent 'luring viewers' model. Role of corporate public relations has become more telling and visible in this process.

Cutting across different political parties and leaders in power, the government's insensitivity to broadcasting and its implications has been obvious all through these years. I can recall five occasions at least when governments could have been more concerned and foresighted, but missed the opportunity. These are only a few glaring examples.

Lost Opportunities

With the government opening up certain mass media support services to hundred per cent Foreign Direct Investment (FDI) without public or even stakeholder consultations or even awareness, the country gave up the minimum and basic conditions that a sovereign nation normally likes to have. This single-stroke decision of the government has been a big blow and responsible for the current status of a confused, or shall we say, messed up

Indian media scene. These services, where hundred per cent FDI was allowed, include advertising, market research, public relations and media planning.

The second lost chance has been the government ignoring a landmark judgement of 1995, where the Supreme Court suggested an independent regulator for broadcasting.[21] Add to this, television operators were not even obliged to abide by certain minimum conditions that any government anywhere makes mandatory, and which print media in India is already submitting to. For television channels, it is as if mere registration in India suffices. This is not short of abdicating a national responsibility on part of a democratic government!

Third, having constituted a public service broadcaster, Prasar Bharati and placing television and radio under its overall control, successive governments have stopped Prasar Bharati from operating professionally and independently to fulfil the objectives for which television was adopted in the first place.

Fourth, taking broadcasting in a casual way, governments have entrusted the Telecom regularity body (TRAI)[22] with the carrier aspects of broadcasting in an ad hoc way. Then, in 2008, the government also entrusted to TRAI resolution of certain uncomfortable or contentious issues such as the case of TRPs. Telecommunication being a central subject, the Union government had been under continuous criticism for some time in the Parliament and outside, and its television policy was the target of left political parties and the opposition, and also a matter of criticism by the larger public for certain deviant programmes of some channels. However, the governments remained unconcerned or insensitive to TRP operations for over a decade – even when public broadcaster, Doordarshan, was adversely affected and pushed to a corner and deprived of its standing and viewership. Even till very recently, the government did not perhaps understand what this actually means.

Fifth, *the government's lack of concern for impact and implications aspect as part of a nation's broadcasting policies and a government's responsibilities is another lost opportunity.* The Indian government has for five decades ignored the fact that there have been many impact studies on television in the USA and UK. This has led to a short-sighted bureaucratic view and ad hoc decisions of successive governments in India.

In this myopic process, television has mushroomed in India as nowhere else in the world with proliferation of channels from all over the world, in a short span of a decade. This has compelled channels to succumb to quick and readymade solutions like TRPs and content formulas in vogue elsewhere. That there are no trained professionals has further facilitated such a process of (haphazard) growth. Despite shortage of content, television has gone for round-the-clock formats, making repetition a virtue and competition a compromise rather than an opportunity in India. As a result, for many viewers, 'seeing is not always believing'. That is how proliferation of news channels, for example, has not commensurately expanded the reach of television. Channel increase has only meant, duplication in exposure to different media. Adoption of TRP and reliance on it also meant that the impact aspects of television was not a concern and priority.

This is how Indian television got into a TRP trap without evolving its own personality and distinct characteristics and moderations that Indian television could have achieved and consolidated over these fifty years.

Content as Differentiator

CONTENTS AND content priorities of television at a macro level of a country, or of a channel at micro level, at any time point, is what distinguishes and also indicates the kind of hold television has on people. *Control and command aspects of television determines the quality of content and content priorities.*

Globally, most strategies of channels to excel and maximise viewership are to do with contents. With boom in the number of channels, the content options are expected to multiply. With privatisation of television, *competition is expected to increase in such a way that it brings relevance, standards* and *quality in programmes and programming.* Of course, competition has increased but in India, it has meant *more of the same content* model. The quest continues to maximise viewership by offering whatever it takes by way of contents and marketing it.

This aspect is relevant as Justice Ranganath Misra, then the Chief Justice of India, observed at a CMS roundtable on Children's Television on 21 November 1998.[1] That we must be concerned about contents of channels and their priorities is because it amounts to 'an undeclared war on an unprepared people', said the observant Chief Justice.

Way back in 2001, I wrote in the *Frontline* fortnightly and the *Economic and Political Weekly* (EPW), articles titled, 'Of Content and Control'.[2] They were about why contents of television channels have *particular character and priorities.* The articles were based on an analysis of contents of some channels of the time. They pointed out that in India, content trends were not so much driven by people's needs as they were for advertising interests and promoting consumerism.

The articles indicated that there was *a power shift in the balance* that was expected of media concerns and interests. From one of *supplementary revenue* in the early years, dependence of channels on advertising had by the turn of the century become one of *supportive* nature and then to that of *sustaining* the very media. Has that trend changed almost two decades later? Despite competition, proliferation and analysis, there has been hardly much change in the content mix in India.

Even news channels in India, for example, devote 35 per cent or more of their telecast time for commercials formally. This percentage has remained at the same level since 2005. There are some channels which tend to devote more than 40 per cent of their time for advertisements. As many as 127 television channels, including news channels, have not complied with any of the TRAI regulations, even after TRAI came up with some prescriptions in 2013.

Table 4: Percentage of Advertisement Time in News Channels (2008-2011)

Year	In per cent
2008	34.0
2009	35.4
2010	35.6
2011	35.4

Source: TRAI consultation Paper (No. 7/2012)[3]

Hardly two per cent of time of *prime time* news bulletins, for example, is devoted for health, education, agriculture, welfare and environment. There has been no change in this respect since 2000 and only a marginal difference recently. Politics, sports, crime, law and order, entertainment and markets account for more than two thirds of the contents of almost all news bulletins telecast in India. These bulletins are supposed to set the agenda of the country and completely miss out on the national needs like regular health information. No wonder the percentage of viewers for news channels has been on the decline, English Channel viewership has declined significantly since 2014 and even Hindi news channels have declined somewhat (as we see in Table 3). And yet there has been a proliferation of news channels, newer news channels coming up in 2017 and 2018. How come? What explains this phenomenon?

A critical look at content priorities of national news bulletins of news channels over a decade-long period make many wonder how television in India has been very far from realities and grassroots.

As TAM's LV Krishnan espouses, during the critical years, television in India was viewed as the 'biggest platform for

Table 5: Percentage of Advertisement Time of Six News Channels (2011)

Channel	In per cent
1	23.3
2	30.4
3	34.5
4	40.4
5	42.0
6	42.1

Source: TRAI Consultation Paper (No. 7/2012) – based on CMS Media Lab Analysis.[4]

the consumer movement', by wooing women first and then children. The extent of dependence on commercials, which in turn linked to viewer ratings, is a syndrome that channels got into. This nexus between advertising agencies and rating activity—echoed by corporate public relations and the conflict of interest so obvious—was never discussed until my *Frontline* and *EPW* articles. CMS's apprehensions in this regard about TRP were eventually confirmed by TRAI guidelines after a decade, in 2013.[5]

The scene in the context of Children's television, for example, has hardly received public attention and the discourse that it deserves. A lesson from our own All India Radio model in the early years was that by involving children at the early age—as the globally accepted *Sesame Street* serial on television reiterates—significant difference can be observed in children's overall growth path. And yet, what have we done with our television?

There are nearly two dozen children's channels (today in 2018). Yes, of course, not one of these channels is Indian (for example, the Discovery group's channels, Cartoon Network and Disney channels for children, which these days transmit in Indian regional languages and at times include programming with made-in-India characters like Bheem and Little Singham).

Nor do any of the channels telecasting in India have original children-involved programmes. And most of these so-called children's channels like Discovery Kids today have more than 15 minutes of product ads in a hour-long programme. The advertisements blatantly lure children to demand the products, be it biscuits or toothpaste.

Until 1994, Doordarshan had one weekly programme for children every afternoon and two on Sundays. By 2001, despite increase in total hours of transmission, there were only three children's programmes in a week, including the weekend. Most children's programmes on other channels were 'imported' or foreign ones—mostly animated films like Doremon—with most having no message of any kind even remotely but dubbed into regional languages. Some of these children's channels (as well as adult channels like the Soni group, Zee group and others) have recently been repeating serials on Hanuman, Krishna, Ganesha, Shiva and such epic characters. TRP has today led to a decline of children's programmes even on Doordarshan.

Of course, children are being used more prominently for and in commercials for promoting consumer brands (like the Bournvita and Complan or Dabur toothpaste ads. They are also used in Adult channels like the Flipkart ad and washing machine or detergent ad). Now, they are also being used in reality shows like the *Indian Idol* and fiercely competitive music shows, all of which are mentored by Bollywood icons, have huge viewerships and 50 per cent advertisement time. While music shows, as such, are not bad per se, the competitions can be hugely stressful for the children and families, the parameters of success they set is Bollywood and not exactly the goals India's visionaries imagined for a young India.

Table 6: Priorities in the Content Trends of Six Bulletins of Telugu News Channels – 2005-2010

ETV2	TV9	NTV	Mahaa TV	Zee 24	Saakshi
Crime	Crime	Politics	Politics	Politics	Governance
Politics	Politics	Crime	Crime	Crime	Politics
Accidents/ Disasters	Social Issues	Governance	Weather	Weather	Accidents/ Disasters
Governance	Human Interest	Sports	Governance	Governance	Crime
Sports	Art/Culture	Art/Culture	Accidents/ Disasters	Human Interest	Social Issues

Source: CMS Media Lab[4]

CMS had tracked on a daily basis most channels in Telugu as the number of channels were the highest, including news channels. An analysis of the trends with specific reference to Telugu for a few years brings out what devastating and deceptive news, the channels delivered. This is what I call the 'tranquilising effect of TRPs'. These years (2005-2010) should be indicative of the state of 'Indian TV' in general. For, these were the years when news channels proliferated, even more in Telugu. More of

Table 7: Trends in Priorities of News Bulletins (Telugu News Channels) 2007-2010

Proliferation of news channels has hardly made any difference!

ETV2			TV9		
2007	**2008**	**2010**	**2007**	**2008**	**2010**
Crime	Politics	Crime	Crime	Politics	Crime
Politics	Crime	Politics	Politics	Crime	Politics
Governance	Governance	Accident/ Disasters	Governance	Governance	Social Issue
Art/Culture	Art/Culture	Governance	Social Issue	Civic	Human Interest
Social Issue	Sports	Sport	Accident/ Disasters	Art/Culture	Art/Culture
Accident/ Disasters		Art/Culture	Sport	Sports	Governance

Source: CMS Media Lab[4]

Table 8: Content Priorities of Telugu News Bulletins (2008-2010)

Long standing news channels (6+ years)		Recent news channels (4 years)		New entrants (<2 Years)	
ETV2	**TV9**	**NTV**	**Mahaa**	**Saakshi**	**HMTV**
Crime	Crime	Politics	Politics	Govt.	Govt.
Politics	Politics	Crime	Crime	Politics	Politics
Accidents/ Disaster	Social	Govt.	Weather	Accident/ Disaster	Social
Government	Human Int.	Sports	Government	Crime	Human Int.
Sports	Art/ Culture	Art/ Culture	Accident/ Disaster	Social issues	Cinema

Source: CMS Media Lab4 – Hyderabad

the same rather than competitiveness or creativity or concerns are evident from the tables in this chapter. The more the competition, the *more of the same* phenomena is evident.

ETV 2 and TV 9 Telugu news channels are each more than 12 years old and have been in a competitive mode from the very outset. And yet, in what way are they different in their content coverage—except that ETV does not carry commercials in between its prime-time news bulletin?

The tendency was to get into the TRP race as the only way to attract advertising by figuring in the ratings. The channels on launch or entry may start with some new initiatives but soon fall back into the same model of programme contents.

More of the same approach of television channels is obvious in their content priorities as was evident from a CMS analysis of 26 Telugu channels during prime years of TRPs. *What has been the contribution of TRPs?* They facilitate channels to claim 'number one' and 'most popular' or 'undisputed' positions in their respective segments. *How can these positions remain the same for a channel for two decades?*

Table 9: Share of News Channels in the Total Viewership – by Age Group

	2007		2008		2009	
	4+ years	25+ years	4+ years	25+ years	4+ years	25+ years
English News	0.7	0.75	0.6	0.62	0.4	0.42
Hindi News	4.8	5.29	4.8	5.36	3.6	4.18
Regional News	2.4	2.92	2.7	3.66	3.6	4.26

Source: TAM6

There is no evidence of commensurate increase in the overall reach of television nor in the overall viewership despite boom and proliferation in the number of channels. In 2002, 27 channels accounted for 80 per cent of the total Telugu viewership, which in 2008, for example, was accounted for by 49 channels. *The viewership numbers remained static*. That is, a myth was created and perpetuated, making no departure from the past and remaining bound to the TRP narrative.

Some realisation of this TRP trap, however, was created among channels once TAM's TRPs were exposed by NDTV and then by TRAI itself. We now need to see whether BARC is going to make a difference. This can be assessed for 2015-2019 and the 2020-2025 periods.

It is obvious from analysis of these television trends that ratings inhibited original Indian creative thinking and plurality aspects and prevented them from coming to the fore in different regions of India as channels were *made to fall in line* because of dependency on advertising. Concern for needs of the people and what is in their interest was not evident. How to attract advertisers and how to draw eye-balls and make TRPs were set up as industry bench-marks and for reliability.

No of Channels that Contributed 80% of Viewership Increase

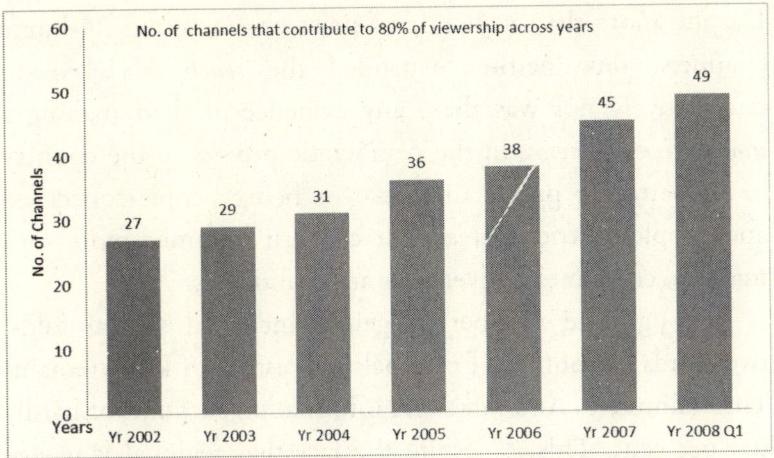

Source: TAM People-meter Systems TG:CS4+ Market: All India Period: 2002-2008 Q1
Fueling media insights that drive businesses
Courtesy: TAM Media Research Pvt Ltd – taken from Shoma Munshi's book.[7]

Content Model

Television in India continues to be known more as an 'entertainer' despite proliferation of 24-hours news channels across the country. The kind of news, verbiage and campaigns channels were preoccupied with all through the decade of 2000-2010 surprises the average media student. In what way did meter-based ratings for a decade help? Did India lack a concern for the communities and creativity so that it could not make use of a powerful visual media to motivate people to unleash the best in them? Was that not a result of too much reliance on TRPs by the channels, the government and the regulators and the sister media? This is the dilemma that I described a decade ago as 'hijacking of Indian television' and channels remaining 'under trap of TRPs'.

The first time that TRPs became suspect was in 2012-2013. This was almost fifteen years after the ratings mania took hold of and began dictating the priorities of channels in India. Despite more than a decade of news channels and 24-hours channels, they neither expanded the *reach* of television cumulatively nor was there any evidence of their making a *qualitative difference* in the democratic process of the country or in bettering public discourse or being people-concerned and people-centric. Instead, the concern remained more with markets, consumers, advertisers and politicians.

Though the number of genres increased several folds, two thirds of content of channels telecasting in India remains 'entertainment'. And news and information account for hardly ten per cent. This is despite the fact that regional language channels have somewhat saved the scene with some experiments and initiatives—as they were not yet or not fully under the grip of TRPs.

Table 10: Viewership Share by Genres

	2012
Kids	6.50%
	6.50
Hindi Movies	12.00%
Hindi GeC	30.00%
Regional GeC	20.00%
Regional Movies	3.65%
	65.65%
English News	0.23%
Hindi News	3.18%
Regional News	2.78%
Infotainment	1.00%
	7.19%
Music	3.00%
Sport	-
Other	16.00%
	19.00%

Source: The Marketing White Book 2014-15[8]

Table 11: The Growth of Indian TV by Programme Genres (2004-2012)

	News					Entertainment		Movies		
	Hindi	English	Business	Regional	Kids	Hindi	English	Hindi	English	Regional
2004	3.7	0.3	0.1	1.2	2.7	24.2	0.7	10.0	1.4	4.6
2005	4.2	0.3	0.4	1.5	4.0	23.6	0.5	9.9	1.1	5.4
2006	4.5	0.5	0.5	1.7	5.8	23.0	0.4	10.5	1.0	5.2
2007	4.8	0.7	0.5	2.4	5.9	22.6	0.3	10.5	1.0	4.7
2008	4.8	0.6	0.5	2.7	5.4	23.2	0.2	11.6	0.8	4.6
2009	3.6	0.4	0.2	3.7	5.5	23.0	0.2	6.5	0.8	5.1
2010	3.4	0.3	0.2	3.5	5.9	26.4	0.1	6.9	0.7	4.7
2011	3.8	0.3	0.1	3.8	6.2	25.5	0.1	7.6	1.0	4.2
2012	3.2	0.2	0.1	3.4	7.0	29.1	0.2	9.0	1.0	4.0

Source: Compiled from TAM India, Globalisation and Television,[9] The Marketing White Book 2014-15, The Indian Media Business[8]

Table 12: Programme Composition of Doordarshan-I Channel % of Programmes

	Nation Network			Regional Services		
	Education	Information	Entertainment	Education	Information	Entertainment
1994-95	28	34	37	39	35	25
1998-99	23	35	42	33	36	31
2006-07	09	33	51	-	-	-

Source: DD annual reports10 '94, '95, '97, '99, 2000, 2003, 2006 and 2007

The years between 2004 and 2012 should have reflected the difference TRPs have made on the content priorities of channels. Viewership of English news had declined markedly, also of Hindi news during this period. Growth of media otherwise, during these years, was higher only in the case of some regional news channels. There was significant increase in the number of regional news channels. Increase in viewership was only marginal in the case of children's channels and the entertainment section of Hindi channels.

Doordarshan

Doordarshan's mandate remained education, information and entertainment all through the years. No change in the policy or objectives were ever indicated otherwise. But between 1994 and 2007, the critical year of TRP's grip on television, there was significant decline in the education content of Doordarshan and increase in the entertainment content. This period was when Star TV (originally a Murdoch group company and now a fully owned subsidiary of 21st Century Fox), whose programmes were rated highest, made its stand in India and pretended to be the benchmark in telecasting. No aspect of education ever formed part of the concern of Star TV during those early years (or even later).

There were impressive examples of content alternatives cutting across entertainment, education and the information sector but no efforts were evident to experiment, as that would have empowered people.

Humlog, Nukkad, Rajini etc. for example, had never adversely effected Doordarshan's viewership as has been sometimes made out. There was enough content available globally and Indian content too that could strategically reach out to more people and even expand viewership and also help empowerment. This 'entertainment-education' model was taken up in India by one or the other entertainment channel (and infotainment channels) *only after* TAM's TRPs came under scrutiny officially in 2012-13.

Another interesting and intriguing aspect is that despite the fact that viewership pattern is distinctly different for news and entertainment channels and between regional channels and others, *the TRP methodology of TAM was uniform week after week and year after year, during those years (1995-2013).*

By switching on and off, of the buttons of meter recordings (presumably)—that is by switching on and off the television set—*programme viewership cannot be measured.* One can just measure *how many are watching television at a particular point in time.* Viewership cannot be given same weightage at the time of news and during the time of a feature film or a serial, for example. There has been no evidence of appropriate change or modification in TRP methodology on when one is to be considered as a viewer of news or a viewer of film. During these two decades, the structure of the meter was changed and was given a new name, the 'people meter'. After 2010, there has been a great deal of technological change in the architecture of the television set, the remote and the mode of telecasting like, digital, live streaming, from cable to DTH to data card etc. that could have improved the reliability of TRPs or 'impressions' (as it is described now). There is no study so far on *to what extent new and upgraded technology has enhanced the reliability of the meter capture of 'actual viewing' of specific television content.*

Basic Infrastructure for Indian Content Model

In the 1990s, when television channels started proliferating, India was not without the much-needed infrastructure for the nation to evolve its own content model for television, distinct from that of the USA.

In fact, Indian feature films were going to 145 countries and India was the largest producer of feature films in the world. India had film production infrastructure in Mumbai, Chennai, Calcutta and there were several prominent production houses with impressive studio infrastructure, long before television's entry. The government's Films Division was producing many news reels and documentaries every week. Even the Children's Films Society had produced or sponsored several feature films which were very relevant for Indian television transmission.

India also had reasonable training institutes of different sizes spread across the country. The Pune Film & TV Institute of India was Asia's sought after acting, production and direction institute which has made a huge difference in the Indian film industry, helping it to be a global industry today (Television was added to its name in the early '70s). Even Jamia Milia's Jamal Kidwai Mass Communication Centre and the Indian Institute of Mass Communication (IIMC) were well established institutes by then.

As early as in 1963, Professor YB Damle of Pune University's Sociology department did research on audio and video media which even the UNESCO called 'an unique study'. The research and evaluation division (1974-6) of IIMC had by then done a range of India-specific studies. Even more impressive were the pre- and post-programme research conducted for SITE (1975-77). In fact, the research model for television undertaken by ISRO,

Ahmedabad, by then was unique and would have contributed a great deal towards Indian television's evolution into an India-specific content model and for the good of the Indian people in a win-win way.

More curiously, before INTAM and TAM came into the picture, ORG was experimenting with a more appropriate methodology for television research, going beyond just the 'reach' dimension which was what INTAM and TAM were concerned about in their meter-based pursuit as that was what their principles (Nielsen and Kantar) had commercialised in some other countries and their corporate subscribers were interested in.

Indian advertising infrastructure was by then much bigger and the world's leading creative body, with laurels both for print and television commercials. For that very reason, by 2000, nearly two dozen Indian agencies were acquired by foreign agencies fully or partly. As a result, today all the top twenty ad agencies in India are controlled by foreign advertising corporates.

By 1992-95, India had more than a dozen software production houses with capability to initiate and produce India-relevant serials or similar programmes imaginatively. Ronnie Screwvala, for example, had 104 television serials in seven languages. Cine Vista and Balaji were the other leading production houses. Realising the potential of Indian software houses, Star TV, for example, acquired more than a quarter of the holdings of Balaji Tele Films which Star gave up, once it no longer needed to depend on Balaji for its own requirements.

Adding to such extensive infrastructure, India had professionals for graphics, animation and a mix of technologies.

Equally important is that all this is at a reasonably low cost, at much lower costs than what the same services would have cost elsewhere. Several Hollywood films are being produced fully or partly in Indian studios, the Ramoji Studio continue to be a state-of-the-art production house for 15 years now. Today Indian animators, sound technicians, cameramen and many others are well-known and well established in Hollywood and foreign channels like the BBC and National Geographics. And, in fact, in the '90s, India was viewed as a country for outsourcing by foreign countries. Until 2010, in India, none of these capabilities were harnessed by television channels to come up with India-relevant content.

By going for a foreign model content, the cost of production of Indian channels was hiked several times, effecting the viability of channels from India.

Prescribing programme priorities in the name of 'consultancy' by rating agencies and the ratings themselves that were put out week after week for certain type or category of contents, serials and sitcoms etc, was one factor that deprived India of an India-specific model of television with its own content.

Nalin Mehta in his brilliant book, *Behind a Billion Screens,*[11] has reminded us that Indian television channels spend by far, the lowest on their actual content. For this he gives three reasons: one, economic, second, government policies, and, third and more importantly, the channels' lack of what I call 'concern' for the needs of the majority of the people of the country and the reluctance to take on the challenge.

As I said a decade ago, television channels could have accomplished what successive governments have failed to do over sixty years. Instead, channels have been repeating even news bulletin after bulletin, as if there is nothing significant and important for people happening around that deserves new content and coverage. Instead of availing the opportunity of diversity, channels tend to work for homogenising content. Instead of taking on socially conscious programmes, channels are busy doling out what 'interests' people with deep pockets. Ratings by TAM had pepped up more of the same type of programming. As Mehta rightly observed in his book, there has been a 'severe crisis of content' and that has deprived television channels in India of an opportunity to create and make the much-needed difference.

Content Concerns of the Country!

Committee after committee of the government in the early years of television in India has warned of the need to gear up on the software front, warned of likely influx of foreign content and its implications to the nation. In fact, for that, one of the committees had even suggested gearing up of our decision-making system. While governments are good to think about, they have no nerve to go about and take directional decisions as well as steering decisions of immediate consequence. This is amply evident even more in the case of television. Even the wisdom of the Supreme Court met the same fate as many of those early insights of the committees on broadcasting. Such a blurred atmosphere helped the TRP culture entrench itself and penetrate television assessment with irreversible implications in a matter of a decade and without coming under serious public scrutiny and debate.

The AK Chanda Committee[12] of 1964-65 had suggested the 'independent corporation' approach for broadcasting in India and this committee was the first to suggest that television (although yet to make an entry) should not be part of *Akashvani* or Radio (AIR). I had an opportunity in 1974 to hear first-hand the kind of debate this committee had about television in India from Mehra Masani, who was the Secretary of the Chanda Committee. She was a Deputy Director General of All India Radio at that time. It took nearly a decade for the government to separate Doordarshan, which meant television, from AIR. The Ministry made Ramesh Chandra, a senior functionary of the AIR, with experience in broadcasting as the OSD for television (which at that time meant Krishi Darshan and a couple of school broadcasts). I had more than a couple of meetings with Ramesh Chandra in 1974 in Akashvani Bhavan on ambitious future plans for television in India.

BG Verghese[13] (George for many) was an amazing personality of many virtues and many leaders in Delhi relied on his wisdom for four decades. As a member of a UNESCO-appointed McBride Commission, his insights on public policy-making were acknowledged as much as he was as an Editor of the *Hindustan Times* (1969-75). All those years, he was consistent that broadcasting should be people-centric and decentralised. He believed in media, particularly broadcasting, for development and as a level player. George, Bhaskara Rao and another amazing personality of the time, Dileep Padgoankar advocated a three-tire broadcasting for India with active participative role of citizens as a part of a draft initiated independently for a Broadcast Bill.[14]

Even the Janata Party government (1978-79) looked for George's advice on television more specifically, when he reiterated that television in India has distinct responsibility and should not get submerged in a western model. He was one of the first members of Prasar Bharati, I had several rounds of discussions with him on this and on other related issues over two decades.

The irony of the Indian public policy-making was that it never relied on its own wisdom and even insights from its own experiences. SITE (1975-76) was a landmark experiment in satellite broadcasting and development communication. No other experiment on use of broadcasting for people's participation and development was ever studied and evaluated as this one-year (1975-77) old project in 2,400 villages spread over different language States. The timing of this experiment at the instance of Vikram Sarabhai was such that its findings could have changed the face of this country, but all that went in vain. Even the Pij TV station in Gujarat was wound up as if deliberately, as it was trying to remind us of a new model of India-specific and appropriate for India television.

Had any of our leaders and planners read any of the reports on SITE, India would have hesitated to go ahead and allow a western model of contents in broadcasting for India. And certainly, we would have preferred *effects* or *impact type* research than going for a viewership rating service. Professor Yashpal, Professor Chitnis, Kiran Karnik and Vinod Agarwal of ISRO's Space Application Centre at Ahmadabad offered a professional 'team' approach for broadcasting rather than a bureaucratic model that we ended up with.

While SITE was under implementation, as an advisor at the Ministry, I had drawn attention to 20 critical issues that deserved to be looked into. These were referred to the ISRO team by the Ministry in the review meeting with Professor Yashpal, and those targets were meant to make sure that India opts for a distinct field research-based content model for television.

PC Joshi[15] was a professor at Delhi School of Economics when he was appointed (1984-85) to head a committee on television software. Vinod Agarwal of SITE was also a member of this committee. The Joshi Committee report of 1985 on software had cautioned of a 'threat from influx of foreign programming'. This warning was described in detail in the report just before satellite television was unleashed in India, with its range of different programmes and before private broadcasters entered broadcasting in a big way. This report was not even remembered a decade later, as it too was shelved like the reports of many other committees. The Joshi report flagged 'the threat faced by the developing nations from the influx of foreign programming' and reminded the government of the need for *Indian character of contents.*

With appearance of Star television on the Indian scene in 1991-92 and talk of many other global players knocking the door of India, the Supreme Court of India in 1995 observed that *airwaves belong to the public* and they should not be used for 'private advantage'. It suggested going for an independent corporation to manage airwaves. Apparently, the apex court had visualised well ahead that foreign influx was going to happen, and profit maximisation was going to be the pursuit. The government had publicly declared its acceptance of the court's judgement and even hinted that it would institute an independent commission.

Retrospectively, we know that political leaders at the helm of affairs wanted the opportunity to handle the matter in a 'case by case' manner. Now we see how politicians created the opportunity for lining their own pockets from these foreign players, by giving each one a case-by-case entry. This is how, growth of television played out in India in a haphazard and unregulated way, without the oversight of a regulatory mechanism. In fact, permissions were issued without even minimum conditions for public disclosures, redressal of public complaints and any kind of restrains on the programme content. CMS even filed (1998) a PIL reminding the government of the Supreme Court judgement.[16]

Shunu Sen was chief of marketing at Hindustan Levers (HLL) then and was viewed as the voice of the corporate world of Mumbai. HLL was one of the top five advertisers in India and a major advertiser globally too. The Ministry of Information and Broadcasting appointed him to head a committee (2000) on positioning and revamping the strategy of Doordarshan. Kiran Karnik[17] of SITE fame and later chief functionary of the Discovery Channel was also a member of the Shunu Sen Committee and helped Sen in drafting the report in 2001. This committee also suggested well-defined identity and positioning and decentralisation in the decision-making of the public broadcaster.

In an interview with Sunetra Sen Narayan, author of *Globalisation and Television: The Indian Experience 1980-2000* (published in 2014), Kiran Karnik[18] argued for what he said from several forums, including from CMS seminars. Karnik argued that the 'presence of transnational broadcasters has contributed to the rise of consumerism in India. The traditional Indian family and its concern with its progeny is being eroded by the instant gratification culture, as purveyed by satellite television'. The Sen Committee, according Narayan, was of the 'opinion that globalisation as represented by the foreign invasion of broadcasting has occurred not only in terms of channels and programmes, but more insidiously in terms of the appearance of foreign themes and values'. He was referring to Star TV and Sony channels more specifically, as *they were being shown in TAM reports as always on the top of the TRP charts week after week, and from the very outset of their launch in India, far ahead of Doordarshan's TRP.*

Based on an analyses of popular prime time soaps (which meant top TRPs) aired on Star Plus in 2000-01, Sunetra Sen Narayan has observed that there was 'a neo-conservative portrayal of women' in these soaps telecast by these two channels. 'There is very little emphasis on female empowerment, once a theme encouraged on DD. The global corporations' portrayal of traditional women (in India) is at variance with the state's objectives of encouraging modernisation and the empowerment of women', Narayan added.[19]

One turning point was Minister VC Shukla's decision to open up Doordarshan for commercials, with no restrains prescribed despite my note against such a model. This set the tone for advertisement-driven privatisation, opening up of the economy and satellite television taking a big leap.

As early as September 2001, I wrote in more than a couple of newspapers, including the *India Television* website, the havoc that the TRP hoax was causing with sample size starting with 400 meters and reaching 4,400 meters for INTAM and 3,500 for TAM. How, even after a decade of coming to India, they were just scratching the surface of the television viewership scene of the country in 2001. Around this time, CMS had explained how a paradigm shift was taking place in the country with TRP measures and the government allowing hundred per cent FDI into media support services of advertising, market research, public relations, and media planning which together were orchestrating the TRPs. There were several questions inside and outside the Parliament about the fallacy of TRPs. But none of this impressed the government. In its wisdom, the government believed it knew better.

It was only after I provoked the Union Minister, Jaipal Reddy, to take cognisance of TRPs and after the CMS round table (2007) with the rating agencies at India International Centre, New Delhi, that the Ministry referred the rating matter to TRAI (in 2008).

One wonders how Star TV and Sony TV serials, however gripping they may have been, could have got such high ratings in India even before the channels had taken roots and spread their reach in countrywide networks. This shows how irrelevant TRP measures actually were.

Turning Point in Content Concerns

Sunetra Sen Narayan is a Professor at the Indian Institute of Mass Communication (IIMC), New Delhi. She examined the transformation of Indian television in the crucial period based on content analysis, archival research and detailed interviews with experts like Kiran Karnik. She pinpoints all the turning points in the evolution of Indian television and how content strategies of foreign channels played a big (havoc) role. In her book,[20] in the chapter, 'the Rise of private television', she narrates how Star TV contents were initially positioned to be on the top of TRP charts. Narayan describes in detail Star TV's origins in India and how for the Star group, relying on family drama and women in soaps and serials had paid off in terms of TRPs. *It was by fuelling 'regressive portrayal' of women that Star TV acquired and retained its premier position throughout the decade (2000-2010).*

Concluding that *content* changed for the worse in 2000, Narayan quoted a media analyst who had said that in spite of having women in lead characters, they were portrayed regressively especially in Hindi television channels.[21] To quote from her book, 'In the 1980s' television, women were shown as striving to break traditional moulds. New millennium television is hell-bent on taking the big leap backwards and transforming the country into a nation of bahus (daughter-in-laws) where marriage is raisin d'être of a girl's existence. Getting married or staying married; these are the only motivations for the female of the species on the small screen... the success of the extended *parivar*, family series seems to have totally blocked the path for avant-gardism and any slice of life's realism'.[22]

What was the government and civil society of the day doing when this is how Star television and several other channels featuring negative serials? Were there any objection or protests? Civil society in India obviously did not realise what showing such serials meant and did not know the mechanism or limit of TRPs. What about the government? It could not be bothered. Overwhelmingly, everyone was in favour. Those who were not did not have a voice. And, content of channels was not monitored or analysed at all by anyone. *More disappointing is the fact that academics of that time never raised a voice against this conservativism. Nor did any university faculty take up any research or analysis to find out what such serials meant, if they were shown throughout India.* It was just a few social activists—

some teachers in Kolkata and Chennai who took out rallies—and Left political party activists who first raised concerns in New Delhi about the 'repressive coverage' of women by some television channels.

In 2007, for the first time, the Minister for I&B took the initiative of having a two-day parley with some 40 activists and researchers and sought their views. SK Arora, then I&B Secretary, lead the discussion for which I was also invited. That led the Ministry to write to TRAI, but that was at the end of 2008. Soon a Committee (led by Amit Mitra of FICCI) was also appointed for future direction on ratings.[23]

The Ministry could have restrained such transmission by issuing an advisory to channels involved in such contentious and callous coverage of women and families. Even such concern by the channels themselves (The Amit Mitra panel was reported in the print media) would have changed the composition and direction of contents telecast. However, by that time, the TRP mania raged. For such a change in content to take place, viewership rating has to be relied upon—at least that was what the TRP promoters made the nation believe. Advertisers and their associates (PR, MR, MP) went along, echoing the TRP mantra.

Advertisers, among them major Indian corporate houses, should have taken some interest to correct the preoccupation of some channels. For, it is their advertising support, of course going by TAM, to these regressive serials that kept the channels going and prompted them to telecast more of such episodes and serials. It is advertisers, whose continued support that made such contents become the model and perpetuated it as some kind of a new order of television.

As Narayan points out, 'The high TRPs garnered by soaps which portrayed women in this fashion, implied that the MNCs and advertisers were backing these programmes in the year 2000'. Narayan, however, did not look into how such serials on women got rated high in the first instance, higher than the other appealing programmes on other channels like Doordarshan with larger and wider network of channels and able to reach out to much larger audiences. Based on these TRPs put out by INTAM and TAM ratings, Star TV claimed it was *the number one Hindi entertainment channel.* Star TV boasted, it telecast '42 out of 46 top programmes in India'. It said, in fact, in April 2001, '34 of the top rated 50 programmes (telecast in India) were from the Star TV stable'.[24]

At that point in 2000-01, how could so many of Star TV programmes be rated higher than, for example, some programmes of Doordarshan? The rating agency probably applied the same 'on-off' ratio that they had put together for the 9 cities they were covering earlier, with around just 4,000 meters. Star was not even beaming into as many cities as Doordarshan in 2000. Doordarshan had the same opportunity of being watched in all cities, in all States and also in rural areas that the rating agency did not assess at all (however, without making that explicit). Star was not even telecasting in many urban areas in States like Bihar, Assam, J&K and the North East States.

Also, it is not clear whether such comparisons were made with specific reference to any *target group* population that advertisers were interested in at that point. For example, if the comparison was limited to 'high end or deep pocket consumers' for whom certain value products held attraction, then rating agencies will come up with programmes shown on channels like Star TV and claim much higher viewership. Whereas, if the viewership comparison encompasses 'general population of TV owning households', then ratings will automatically be different even in a given 'market' or city. Surprisingly, Doordarshan's national channel never found a place among the top ten most-watched Hindi general entertainment channels in (urban and rural) viewership matrix, though actually its reach at that time made it the most viewed channel and its programmes the most-viewed programmes.

Things had not changed much in 2015. What explains that, even after BARC's claim of taking into account television viewership in all States of the country and its data representing rural India, Doordarshan's ranking has declined further? Against 82.66 million 'impressions' (viewers) of Doordarshan, Star Plus was in 2015 shown as having 706.324 million impressions.[25] This at a time and in a year when there were nearly 800 channels to see and to view any of Star TV channels, one had to subscribe both in the case of cable and DTH.

In 2018, most of Doordarshan channels can still be viewed freely and directly, with or without Cable/DTH connectivity. It is not rocket science to understand, even the poorest of the poor can be a DD viewer and only people with money can subscribe to Star, and it can in no way have the number of viewers Doordarshan has in a nation of one billion plus, and where television is still out of reach, due to lack of electricity and roads, if nothing else. Not to forget, community televisions in remote areas do not subscribe to Star channels, but these communities too are television viewers.

Then there are no benchmarks as to trends in viewership

habits in rural India. Are there any seasonal trends? Is viewership during peak agriculture season different from that of summer weeks? But the TAM ratings were uniform all through and from the very outset of Star TV, when the number of cities covered were only a few and the number of metered TV households were hardly a couple of thousand.

Research for a Proactive Role of Channels?

Research and feedback in creative fields, as in the case of media, is expected to come up with new alternatives apart from course corrective ideas and interventions. Even more so with syndicated research reports, as they are available to all players simultaneously. TRPs were promoted as syndicated service (although with differential subscription). TRP was expected to be a level player in the television scene and, at the same time, TRPs were expected to prompt competitiveness in an open market scenario. Can we find any such evidence, with channels showing a particular kind of soap operas over the last two decades? Neither was competitiveness, nor quality served because TRP became the currency that channels depended on and advertisers went ahead accepting and availing TAM's TRP as a reliable yardstick and benchmark. All that without any transparency and open meets of subscribers to TRP service. (When ORG first introduced the concept of syndicated reports in 1968-70, a subscribers' meet was an annual feature.)

Television in India witnessed unprecedented growth in the previous decade. Channels proliferated and mushroomed all across the country. They multiplied in every genre and the numbers of genre too increased. In such a scenario one expects new and original content and of different scope and structure.

But an analysis of contents by categories do not indicate any such distinct growth. On the contrary, the growth saw more of the same kind of contents, programmes and priorities, as if there were some external limits or restrains on competition when, the last two decades have been free from any national policy framework in India on broadcasting or on television.

This more of the same trend has been evident in three different contexts – news, children and women.

When round the clock news channels emerged and mushroomed in every State, one expected a variety and differentiation in the extent of news coverage, its scope, structure and of course even in terms of reliability, relevance of news channels and news stories. *But what has actually happened?* The kind of competitiveness between channels has led to threatening implications for the very credibility of news channels and news bulletins. As a CMS field report indicated at the height of that growth a decade ago, the situation 'seemed no longer believable'.[26] Even more devastatingly, the growth that news channels had added to the total viewership of television was only marginal. The extent of repetitions of news has increased in news channels. Even the same news bulletin repeats certain footages again and again. A CMS analysis had earlier indicated that the 24-hour news telecast idea has not rejuvenated or even changed the image of television as an entertainer. Consequently, in this decade, the extent of news component in 24-hour news channels have declined by thirty per cent in the first ten years of round- the-clock news channels.

Some of the children's programmes on All India Radio are still recalled positively by some for the opportunity they provided to children to better their creative faculties. Even

Doordarshan had some original children's programmes initiated locally. But that was more than two decades ago. It is well known that children watch television up to four hours on weekends and that a significant per cent of total viewers of television in India continue to be children. What kind of children's programmes are available tailored for or of special interest to children in India? Of course, the number of children's channels have multiplied and TAM's TRP says that a significant per cent of children (of 4+) too were engaged in pushing the on and off buttons on the meter in their household (and now even 2 years+ can do that!). The question is whether any new, local and participative children's programmes have been initiated that one has talked about in the previous years? The TRPs were more for the old epic stories of India (*Krishna, Bheem, Hanuman* etc.) in an animation/cartoon format.

TRPs have apparently helped advertisers to reach children with old and new brands and new products and brands involving behaviour change and life style ideas (like on the Discovery Kids channel). Research and feedback were expected to help come up, particularity in a competitive scenario, with new, original and empowering contents. What evidence do we have that proliferation of channels has helped children of India in any breakthrough way other than in helping promote consumption behaviour and brand preferences? TRPs apparently have not contributed significantly even in this regard. Discovery and National Geographic channels, however, have in more recent years changed the scenario a little bit.

Let us look at the kind of programmes women view according to TAM and the kind of serials and programmes that have mushroomed to woo viewership among women.

That women constitute a significant per cent of total viewers is well known. But what is not known is that original new programmes have not come up for women, as research is expected to facilitate. Of course, programmes on kitchen and cooking have mushroomed and have become popular, so also 'leisure time skills' programmes. But in the serials that were made popular by TAM's TRPs, have we seen any thematic change or correctives even after fifteen years after they were made out to be all-time popular shows?

It is more of the same that is dished out for women despite proliferation of channels, increased competition, and a regime of TRPs. It was quite obvious by early 2000 that the so-called 'Indian TV' has come under siege of TRP and it was supporting a particular content model, directly and indirectly. Consequently, the country missed an opportunity to evolve a more appropriate country-specific content option and a model that caters and supports the interests of the people of the country.

Ahmadabad Wave!

The decade of 1965-75 in particular had witnessed a wave of ideas and institutions in Ahmadabad. Thanks to the Ambalal Sarabhai family in Ahmadabad-Baroda, more specifically, Vikram Sarabhai, for his ideas cutting across community service, future concern, management studies, fundamental research, designing etc. These have led to founding of new institutes for the first time in India. Operations Research and its applications was Sarabhai's one such brilliant idea. The Indian Institute of Management, the Physical Research Laboratory, the National Designs Institute and a dozen other institutes have sprung up in this west coast city. With Vikram Sarabhai becoming Chairman of the Indian Space Research Organisation (ISRO) in 1969, and his untimely death in 1971, no doubt the country was deprived of more such institutions.

Although not established as an independent outfit, he ensured that ORG acquired that standing despite being a Sarabhai group activity in support of diversified family-controlled industries. Big industries consider market intelligence as confidential and will not share it with competitors. However, ORG went ahead to take to syndicated market research reports based on its retail audit of drug outlets, household toiletries etc. It so happened, many big and small enterprises in India needed the information and were willing to pay fixed rates for a syndicated research report. One concern behind all these efforts was to take the country to the next level of all-round development by bringing in state-of-the- art management tools and technologies. It was because of such a vision and concern that ORG emerged as a pioneer market research agency and in no time, became the fountain-head of not only market research but socio-economic and media research.

It was Sarabhai's vision and mission that television should change the face of India and leapfrog on its development saga that led to the first successful televised education experiment in the world, SITE. Direct to home (DTH) television, a decade later, was more a commercial avatar of Sarabhai's SITE. It was lack of similar concern and imagination in the government that India missed an opportunity of becoming the global leader in mass communication. What followed after the Pij station was closed was a TRP coup.

One needs to know the backdrop for TRPs, which

unfortunately most people in government did not know and do not know even in 2018, after all the exposes. The only two people interested were IK Gujral and Jamal Kidwai, Minister and Secretary, of the Ministry of Information and Broadcasting who wanted to know whether television with an Indian personality could be developed. For that a committee, with Chitnis of ISRO, Vinod Aggarwal, an anthropologist also of ISRO, and PC Joshi, an economist with social concerns, was appointed by the Ministry.[27] This committee report never received any attention. Even the field research reports of ISRO (with Yashpal, Chitnis, Vinod Aggarwal, Kiran Karnik, Bhatia) on SITE were not followed up. Instead, an irrelevant television rating points scheme (TRP) gained currency. This backdrop needs to be reiterated here again to remind us of the initiatives taken and opportunities missed.

The Decade of Paradigm Shift

THE DECADE of 1991-2001 was a turning point for television in India. On account of what happened during this period, quantitatively India boomed, but qualitatively 'Indian television' failed to meet any kind of assessment. How? Why? There was a transformation all across the broadcast scene. In these years, the transformation had embraced an outdated broadcast model but was adopted as a 'better option' for the future of a brilliant and creative people. The transformation was not for realising what *WE THE PEOPLE* of the country want and aspire for! That is what one gets when things get multiplied and quantitatively scaled up overnight, as if more is merrier even when it is more of the same.

The decade was packed with quick developments. Three

dramatic things had happened during the decade which changed the very scope, structure and systems of television, never before visualised and so swiftly or abruptly!

Privatisation, globalisation and satellite broadcasting happened parallelly, without any preparations and precautions. Yes, each of these national policies, had irreversible impact on Indian broadcasting, as the then Chief Justice, Rangnath Misra had pointed out.[1] Two other developments too changed the very character of that process. The first one was opening up of critical media support services for hundred per cent foreign participation. The second development was adoption of the regressive way of instant rating—of how many were there in front of a telly—an assessment limited to numbers, as an yardstick by themselves in a stand-alone way.

What is astonishing was that governments (there were six Ministers for I&B during the decade, with no one holding the portfolio for even three years continuously during the ten years) pretended to be blind. This meant, the government remained insensitive all through the decade to what broadcasting, specifically television, meant to the nation and hundred per cent foreign investment into critical services meant to the mass media of the country and their concerns and priorities.

This took place even after witnessing what happened in the previous few years with *Ramayana*, *Mahabharata* and *Sri Krishna* serials on Doordarshan. These serials signalled the kind of new heights that viewership could peak to and how people could be galvanised (or provoked) overnight. People also loved the serials like *Humlog*, *Buniyad*, *Nukkad*, *Udaan* etc. Based on field study and CMS workshops around the country, a 1996 book on *Social effects of Mass Media in India*[2] detailed what kind of change television was causing, particularly in women, children and the family system. If the government was not sensitive to a landmark judgement of the Supreme Court on broadcasting (1995),[3] could any proactive initiatives be expected from the government? Some public criticism and Questions in the Parliament started only after 2004.

In 1998, TAM formally got registered in India as a private limited company with AC Nielsen and Kantar as principle and sole promoters. Until then, Nielsen had operated as ORG-Marg, as the front and television rating company, going by name INTAM, as if the rating was by an Indian concern.

The idea of TRP had constrained (Yes) the scope of television in India in an irreversible way and regressively. All this happened during this decade with no one aware and concerned about what it all possibly meant. Curiously, the government did not even take notice of such significant intervention with rating services by someone with no known credentials in India at that point in time.

Doordarshan should have been more sensitive and aware of what and how ratings were being conducted for so long (1993-2008). The channels had the option (for a short period of less than two years) to choose between two TRP reports parallelly, INTAM and TAM. Both were of the same irrelevance, having the same inadequacy in their methodology and involving similar kind of loopholes in administering the meters. And yet no one had raised this as an issue of any concern, not even Doordarshan. Even academics did not. No wonder then that INTAM and TAM merged in 1991 to save themselves from the embarrassment of inconsistencies in the findings and increasing number of posers from public, subscribers and the select media.

Public service broadcaster Doordarshan had a much larger network which was decentralised, with nearly 1500 transmitters, over 30 channels and 60 studios. By the year 2000, Doordarshan had a reach of well over 225 million households because of its presence in terrestrial, cable and satellite channels. The content options available, however, were not the same. The range of programmes of different genre available on Doordarshan channels were unmatched. And yet INTAM and TAM were publicising higher viewership for programmes of foreign satellite channels (which were hardly a couple of years old by then and their reach was limited to deep-pockets) based on a sample from 29 major cities with only a couple of thousand meters in all to track 'chances of seeing' their respective TV screen at any given time point.

The chance was based on a 'push-on, push-off' button on a meter (set top box). Children of 4 to 9 years of age in a household can operate this box. Until 2000, no one even talked of meter-based viewership. I began writing on the subject in 2001, and then got a meter produced locally (by ECIL, Hyderabad, instead of importing from Canada or South Africa by paying import duties).

No one questioned the research (methodology, sample size, selection procedure, representative character, criteria for viewership compilation, score system and the way the ratings were used and publicised as) aspect of the service, more specifically about the kind of difference television-watching or watching any particular channel or even a particular programme or an episode made. The general public definitely did not know what the news media was reporting about viewership to channels or on what basis. Nor was there any effort on the part of INTAM and TAM to sensitise even television-owning households, make them know how the information collected from households owning television was being used, by whom, even for what purpose and who uses the so-called findings. Since this ignorance suited advertising agencies, they too did not raise an issue. With such passivity in the country, TRP soon became the accepted benchmark, with implications for priorities of television channels of the country.

Thus, the decade 1991-2001 signalled a paradigm shift in the very direction of public communication operations of the country and their priorities in an irreversible way and changed the very lifestyles of people, and relationships and value orientations. And yet these aspects were never looked into or studied by any of the stakeholders or by any independent voices.

Policy that Changed the Course of Media

Table 13: Top Advertisers

Reckitt Benckiser	Pepsi
Cadburys India	Heinz
Marico	Brittania
Emani	Oread India
GSK	Johnson & Johnson
Prefaltic	

Source: N Mehta[4]

Table 14: The Top 13 Advertisers on TV-Corporates

1	Hindustan Lever	8	Ponds
2	Rickett	9	Loreal India
3	Cadbury India	10	Smith Kline Beecham
4	ITC	11	Bharati
5	Procter & Gamble	12	Marico
6	Coco Cola India	13	Samsung
7	Colgate Palmolive		

Source: Vinita Kohli Khandekar[5]

Based on volume of advertising of time

MR (Market Research)

In due course, advertising agencies themselves took to research with competitive advertising gaining ground. But that was mostly to do with pre-testing ad themes or ad copies and campaign strategies. Later, analytical studies in that context acquired demand to justify campaign budgets. However, with multiplication of media options, within and across mass media, specialisation and scale of research opportunities led to floating of market research outfits formally, but these continue to be associated with advertising agencies.

Although ORG (Operations Research Group) had working relations with many advertising agencies, it had 'Shilpi' as a sister advertising agency, operating separately but within the Sarabhai group. The Indian Market Research Bureau (IMRB) sprang up on the Indian scene some years after ORG, as an Indian affiliate of the British Market Research Bureau and affiliated to HTA (Hindustan Thomson Advertising Agency) which was also an affiliate of the UK-based Thomson Advertising Agency. *By 1980, in India there were more than a dozen market research agencies with ORG and IMRB leading. However, surprisingly, by early 2000 there were no major market research agencies owned by Indians* (for the same reason as in the case of the advertising agencies). Even the government today relies more on and engages foreign MR corporates, and not the few Indian ones that are there, as if foreign conglomerates understand India better and are more reliable!

From out of these foreign market research firms, media planning and rating and opinion survey functions and enterprises were carved out with increase in business turnover in each case. They were operating as if they were independent and not in a conflict of interest with other players, supporting or endorsing each other's services for market domination.

Public Relation

Public relations (PR) was a core service of advertising agencies until the 1990. This function was floated as a separate corporate service. And with influx of foreign corporates, the function acquired special weightage—with managing the media and manipulating specific news media becoming the core of their business. The 2G telecom controversy (2013-14) revealed the kind of role public relations corporations play. The Neera Radia[6] scam unravelled gripping stories of PR corporates. By 2000, the top dozen PR corporates operating in India were owned by a top foreign PR company. *PR corporates in India are all foreign-owned or controlled.* Even most individual PR consultants work mostly through foreign associate(s). It was these PR professionals who backed ratings, endorsed and promoted TRP as a reliable criterion.

It is not easy to prove that major shareholding corporates are interconnected in their various entities of ad agencies, market research organisations, public relations companies and media planning and rating agencies. Even today, because mergers, takeovers and bifurcations take place so often, one cannot easily pin down the interconnection.

In 2006-07, when Union Minister Jaipal Reddy asked me whether I could brief him on the origins of TRP in India, I tried for a fortnight to trace who had the controlling rights and specify stakeholders of TAM. *The government, we found, had no records, no documentation.* In such a situation how could accountability be pinned, had there been a need?

For any such rating activity, the nature of fixing the kind of meters in the households and tracking what was going on there has to have registration in India. The monitoring agency has to be responsible for what is being monitored and how the findings are compiled and used. The agency has to be answerable to someone in India. *At that time (even in 2007), no authority of the government or functionary in I&B Ministry was seized of this particular activity.* It was not merely a commercial activity, it involved monitoring and prescribing certain priorities and yardsticks and priorities of the country as well. Television channels were at least registered, and down linking and up linking required government permissions.

TRAI entered the scene much later and much after TRP had become the omnipresent barometer for television channels in India.

An analysis of the trends and a critical retrospective of past functioning indicates that foreign controlled advertising, market research and PR agencies were the 'door men' or launch pads for the global consumer industry and facilitators for foreign broadcasters to enter and become dominant players in the Indian market. For them, TRP was an 'instrument' and part of their marketing strategy. They managed TRPs so that these became the industry currency or yardstick, not just for viewership, but to influence content priorities and programming in order to change the lifestyles of the average Indian, although the idea of such rating was initiated as a support function for advertising strategies and media planning. Since penetration into news media was not possible directly, next best or may be, an even better option was to get control over these various support services of advertising, market research, public relations, media planning, viewership rating and opinion surveys in India. Thereby, this TRP enabled control of both content and the very viability aspect of TV channels in India.

What should intrigue us more is that despite the National broadcaster, Doordarshan, being adversely and unfairly affected, no one in the government looked into the visible contributing factor of the TRP phenomena. This was for over a period of ten years (1990-2000) during which period there were three or four different Union governments, half a dozen Ministers of I&B and as many Secretaries of the Union Ministry.

Even more intriguing at that time was that when I went to the Minister, KP Singh Deo, Secretary Bhaskar Ghosh and the Director General S Basu of Doordarshan and explained to them how DD was losing out by default, they did not want to acknowledge this as a fact and were not willing to even examine the matter. It was some time later, after my discussion with them that I came to know that DD's DG, Basu, was already by then in negotiations with Murdoch and he soon joined as the CEO of Murdoch enterprises, to expand the Star TV channels in India. Basu took with him some senior DD officials as well as storm troopers to influence the government, others also to induce without losing time the successful authors of DD serials and convince them to write serials for Star TV networks. *A case of internal sabotage which no one in the media talks about,* thanks to Basu's influence with the politicians, cutting across parties.

FDI into Media Support Services

A decade before the TRP system took off in India, I went to the AC Nielsen HQs in New Jersey in 1981-82, as president of India's first market research leader, Operations Research Group (ORG).[7] By then ORG had already taken to regular monitoring of commercials on television channels and periodic viewership studies. I was on an exploratory visit to leading market research agencies for possible collaboration. The vice-president of overseas operations of *AC Nielsen told me that they do not consider Indian market as a 'critical mass' for them to consider any such interest in India.* He further indicated that the size of television market (in terms of advertising outlays) was not big enough and also that the market was too segmented and diffused.

Soon thereafter, what happened in India in the name of economic reforms was that the Government of India allowed 100 per cent foreign direct investments into critical support services to media enterprises. (Perhaps because no FDI could be allowed into mass media, more specifically, the news media, without a debate on the floor of the Parliament.) These services continue to directly and indirectly determine the scope and size of the media industry itself in the country even today. The government decision to allow 100 FDI was neither publicly debated nor did the Parliament take note of such a crucial decision of far-reaching consequence. *Allowing 100 per cent foreign direct investment into these critical services has turned out so devastating that it was a turning point and beginning of the slipping out of these services from Indian control (and hence no India concerns).* These services—as in the case of advertising agencies, market research, public relations and media planning corporates and rating agencies—too branched out from market research and advertising businesses.

I described these different functional agencies in 1999 when I first analysed the media scene in a report called the 'New Gatekeepers of Media'.[8] In the earlier decades, sub-editors and other desk journalists in news media were described as 'gatekeepers'. Much earlier, they were also described as 'hidden persuaders'. But today they are no longer hidden except that their ultimate linkages are not transparent.

The advertising agency business, for example, determines the extent of support to media in general and what individual media outlets get specifically. In fact, their very survival depends on advertising support which is determined by advertisers and *their perceptions of markets and the methodology* followed for media planning and budget making. Advertising agency business in the earlier years included media planning, market research and public relations. But once these businesses were opened up for FDI, each of those functions was floated as separate entities.

Lintas, which was an in-house advertising agency of consumer (toiletries) product marketing agency, Levers became Hindustan Lever. When it was required to register in India, Richardson became Hindustan Richardson and many other such consumer and marketing corporates established their local stand in similar manner. Their principles are traded in New York and London Stock Exchanges. Most other advertising agencies until that period were Indian. By 1996-97, there were only a couple of the top 20 advertising agencies that were Indian. By 2010 there were hardly any left, with the fall of RK Swamy much earlier, and the last Indian agency to yield was Mudra Advertising Agency.

Market Research

Market research in India was initiated as an in-house activity in the early sixties, not so much as a specialised service, until the one in the Sarabhai group was repositioned as Operations Research Group (ORG), as a support activity to their pharma, textiles, home products etc. by inducting statisticians from the Indian Statistical Institute, Calcutta. With the taking up of country-wide retail audit-based studies which were later offered as syndicated services, ORG emerged as a specialised outfit. IMRB and later BMRB emerged when Ranjit Chib and Tito Ahluwalia of BMRB returned from London to start MARG and MRAS, both of them focussed on studies in support of corporates. From the very outset, they enjoyed certain patronage of global corporates and they were not competitors.

Advertising

Advertising receives boost from growth in the economy and in an increasing proportion, to growth in the GDP. More directly, the boost comes from the per cent of sales spend on advertising. Proliferation of product categories, where competition is intense between ever-increasing number of brands and growth in sales of these category of products in particular, sustains the media. This is particularly the case with television channels and their viability.

Table 15: Ratio of Advertising Spend to Sales, 1990

High (>5%)	Low (<3%)	Medium (3-5%)
Shampoos	Shaving Cream	Face Cream/acne preparations/whiteners
Chocolates	Toilet soap	Coffee
Scourers	Washing powder	Beverages
Washing soap detergents		Milk powder/weaning foods
Tea		Analgesic Tablets
Shaving System/Blades		Hair dressings
		Talcum powder
		Tooth paste/powder

Source: ORG Data base (up to 1990)[9]

Table 16: Advertising Revenue

Years	Rs	Billion
	TV	Total
2008	82	221
2009	88	228
2010	103	266
2011	116	300
2012	125	327
2013	139	362
2014	156	409
2015	180	471
2016	207	542
2017(est.)	240	630

Source: Marketing White book.[10] (p.150)

In 2016, Rs 200+ billion was involved in all, in advertising outlays on television out of a total of over Rs 550 billion. It was to facilitate and justify allocation of these outlays among various media at macro and micro level that advertising agencies and media planners sought and seek quantitative yardsticks. That was how they went about for a measurement mechanism by way of readership (NRS) and viewership surveys (TRP).

A much higher per cent of sales turnover is spent on advertising by consumable products/brands. And this per cent has been on the increase since 1990, because a higher per cent

Table 17: Top 10 Super Categories in TV % Share

		2010	2011	2012
1	Food & Beverage	14	13	14
2	Personal Care / Hygiene	13	13	12
3	Services	6	7	7
4	Hair care	5	5	5
5	Personal Accessories	-	5	5
6	Telecom	4	3	3
7	Auto	4	3	4
8	Banking Finance	3	3	-
9	Household Products	-	3	-
10	Personal Health Care	3	3	-
11	Building, Land	-	-	3

Vanita Kohli Khandekar (p.142) *The Marketing White Book* 2014-15 (p149).[11]

of budgets are allocated for television and tariff of channels has been increasing even more, going by the ratings of TAM. The way the number of brands of these consumable products in the market have increased is yet another effect of television advertising. For example, the number of brands of popular and premium soaps in shops have trebled between 1985 and 2000 and the trend has continued thereafter. So is the case with

Table 18: Proliferation of Brands of Selected Consumer Products

Product Category	1985	1990	2000
Shaving Systems	5	9	21
Detergent cakes/bars	32	38	140
Popular soaps	33	51	140
Premium soaps	57	80	170
Shampoos	23	50	100
Mosquito repellent	14	26	40
Sanitary napkins	18	26	35
Refined edible oil	108	116	150
Antiseptic cream	16	22	90

Source: Completed with ORG Data base[9] of '90s.

brands of most advertised consumer product categories.

The share of these consumable product groups in the total TV advertising has remained at the same level despite increase in the number of product/service categories of advertisers on television. Even the top ten marketing companies retained their share despite emergence of several new, including of Indian, marketing companies. More than three fourth of advertising outlays on television were for news channels and what is budgeted for entertainment programmes was hardly ten per cent of total advertising outlays.

Table 19: Ad Outlays and Viewership Shares

Channels Category	Share in Advertising Outlays in percentage	Share in Viewership (2012) in percentage
General Entertainment	5.45	50
Movies	3.3	17
Kids	2.8	3
Business	2.1	?
News	84.4	7

Source: *White Book*[12]

How come, with hardly ten per cent of total viewership of all genre, three-fourth of advertising outlays on television went to news channels? And, hardly ten per cent of advertising outlays were for entertainment (including film-based) when their share in total viewership was more than two thirds?

Theoretically and logically, advertising agencies and media planners are expected to put their money where there is viewership. And that is where the ratings are expected to guide and facilitate. And TRPs are a motivating factor for their budget outlays.

How come, that was not the trend in India in the wake of TRPs? Does this mean that 'TRP' was used more to sustain the viability of 24-hour news channels, even though they were not adding up to viewership? If that was the case, why TRPs at all? Because it amounts to relying on *subjective criteria as was the practice of allocating Ad Outlays before the TRP regime*. And yet, ad agencies and advertisers stood by TRPs! Why?

This is something that I have tried to update myself on and ascertain the logic from the leaders of the advertising community. No other explanation comes forth other than that of the *hold on public opinion* contentious issues have, which means, news channels have.

Regulator TRAI had notified in 2013 an ad-cap restricting advertisements to 12 minutes per hour between 7 pm and 10 pm, 10 minutes of commercial and up to two minutes of channels promotion. The channels themselves are obligated to report status in this regard to TRAI quarterly. An analysis of these reports by TRAI for 2016 (for June-Sept, March-June) brought out that 127 general entertainment channels showed more than prescribed time cap. That is more than 12 minutes per hour. This number was as high as 137 channels earlier – almost all Hindi channels aired more than 12 minutes' time per hour for advertisements. Some channels, as many as 23 news channels, had availed much higher time for commercials than what was prescribed by TRAI. The TRAI order in this regard was even questioned in the courts.

Table 4: Percent of Advertisement Time in News Channels (2008-2011)

Year	Commercial time
2008	34.0
2009	35.4
2010	35.6
2011	35.4

Source: CMS Media Lab, P N Vasanti 2016[13]

Table 5: Percentage of Advertisement Time of Six News Channels (2011)

Channel (Name not given)	In Per cent
1	23.3
2	30.4
3	34.5
4	40.4
5	42.0
6	42.1

Source: CMS Media Lab, P N Vasanti 2016[13]. P.31-32

This discussion indicates that despite TRPs, subjectivity in advertising outlays continues. TRPs are more to justify the budgets and allocations. But even more, they were to influence content priorities and/or promote 'deviant behaviours' for viewer loyalty.

Advertising Driven Ratings

More than two decades ago, as a paradigm shift was on anvil in Indian media scene, I had explained how the 'new gatekeepers' have emerged to influence the content priorities of the media. These new gatekeepers, armed with TRPs, matter far more today than the readers and viewers. These new gatekeepers include advertising agencies, market research outfits, media planners and public relation corporates. Rating agency is the brain child of these new gatekeepers. Later, in 1995 I published a paper, 'Mass Media and Marketing Communication' where I argued that 'mass media' has become more of 'marketing media'.[14]

With the structure of each of these media support functions undergoing visible change after 1991, they have become even more active, as if media are no longer 'hidden persuaders' but are out blatantly and even formally. As a result of the current 'market-view of India' by investors into India, foreign advertising agencies have tied up or acquired control of Indian advertising agencies. By the end of 1990s, most of the top twenty advertising agencies in India, accounting for nearly 80 per cent of advertising outlays through television in particular, had become foreign controlled by majority holding. Interestingly, by early 2000, top ten market research outfits accounting for nearly 90 per cent of market research in India too were foreign as they entered India directly or by taking over an existing Indian enterprise. So also the public relations corporates by around the same time (by whatever nomenclature they were known). This process was smooth as many of the advertisers were already clients or users of the service of these agencies in other countries, in the USA more specifically. It is the same multinational corporates who have significant interests in all these four support functions. Together, in a tango, their common interest and pursuit has been to pep up consumerism and a new lifestyles of 'spend more' and 'consume more' markets.

As much as 45 per cent of revenue from TAM's service was paid by media agencies and 55 per cent by the TV networks. A decade later, this has become less than one third only from the advertisers and around 60 per cent from the channels. They all are engaged in promoting TRP services with the help and special efforts of public relation expertise. Star TV's main source of revenue in India was advertising that accounted for 70 per cent of revenue. To hold on to such level, Star needed ratings and has to remain on the top of the ratings. And, it did manage that position at the very outset of the TRP-led 'rat race'.

Table 20: The Top 20 Creative Advertising Agencies-(2015)

1.	Ogilvy. (1)	11.	Dentsu (17)
2.	Lowe Lintas (3)	12.	Creative Lab Asia (16)
3.	J Walter Thomson (2)	13.	Publicis (15)
4.	McCann world group (4)	14.	Saatchi and Saatchi (12)
5.	Taproot Dentsu. (5)	15.	Grey (14)
6.	FCB Ulka (13)	16.	Interface (20)
7.	Leo Burnett (7)	17.	BBH
8.	DDB Mudra (6)	18.	RK Swamy BBDO (9)
9.	BBDO India (11)	19.	Soho Square
10.	Contact (8)	20.	Wueden Mennedy

Source: ET Brand Equity[15] April 27, 2016
(The figure in bracket was their rank in 2014)

A couple of US-based ad corporates, like the Leo Group, BBD, each has acquired more than one (or associate) competing ad agency in India. These top twenty advertising agencies in India, account for nearly three-fourth of advertising spending in India. The last two truly India ad agencies were RK Swamy and Mudra. The principles of these agencies are outside India and their clientele include many multinationals with interests in India, which also means preference to follow the model which includes reliance or support to the rating system of television by Nielsen and Kantar.

The idea of measuring viewership was mooted by advertising agencies and advertisers to justify advertising budgets and campaign strategies. And also to facilitate media schedules and planning strategies (not media development). The idea of quantifying and syndicating services, like ratings, was to cater to the needs of the advertising community, not so much in the larger interest of serving consumers or viewers of the country. With serials and sitcoms becoming dominant category seen, as in the western countries or even more, the design for ratings with meter had become a business proposition and the same model was adopted in India. *The design of methodology availed for TRPs in India by itself do not offer insights for programme strategies and content priorities of channels, whereas they are being used more for that purpose by channels on their own or in collaboration with the rating agency itself.* That was how the revenue of rating agency from channels was more than fifty per cent. The other revenue being from advertising agencies. That was how ratings have become promotional avenues for channels and even for individual serials and programmes. With increase in the 'sponsored category' of contents of channels, and programme outsourcing becoming a business opportunity, the *ratings* have acquired a differentiating standing in that process as a yardstick and bench mark. And for channels and advertising agencies, ratings have become handy to market 'time segments' as prime time and the like, and justify tariffs and maximise revenues. In the process, the more the dependence of channels on commercials, the more their vulnerability to TRPs and specialised role of media planners to convert this into a business opportunity.

At the outset, until mid-1970, market research, media planning and public relations were the functions mostly of adverting agencies. With National Readership Surveys opening up opportunities in a quantified way and field surveys becoming more regular, structured and syndicated market research has been carved out as a distinct separate business activity.

But some agencies operate in tango, for example IMRB remains a subsidy of the advertising agency, Hindustan Thomson (HTA). With media planning becoming a quantitative exercise, media executives floated media planning as a specialised function and then as a profit centre or business enterprise. Public relations too has similar origin. Even if they operated with a separate identity, close links were kept up between them and advertising agencies. The principles may be the same overseas in some cases as in the case of TAM (WPP), the world's largest advertising and marketing service agency where Martin Sorrell's Kantar group and Group M are the principle. WPP's full name is Wire and Plastic Products (WPP) and the British entrepreneur Sorrell began as a defence contractor and then got into wire shopping baskets, until he is now one of the world's richest men owning most of the high-profile advertising and market research companies; he owns three-fourths of the world, one can say.[16] These differently operating Sorrell corporates work in tandem.

Since principles of TAM rating agency in India are AC Nielsen and Kantar who themselves, being top five MR agencies in the US, are active stakeholders in advertising, market research and public relation functions, ratings have become more a 'joint exercise' for their own win-win opportunity. Imagine a joint Indo-US naval exercise in the Bay of Bengal with a dozen US warships in Indian waters. The purpose of all such joint exercises are to develop capabilities for a country conquest. Ratings were positioned as a profit-making business venture, in a supporting way or in a scratching-eachother's-back way or supporting each other's interests. What is their common interest? Consumerism, of course, in the long run and support eachother's interests in the short term. Consumerism sustains each of them. Which means promoting brands, life styles, supporting markets including stock markets and serving advertisers. Six top market research firms in the USA, with interest in advertising, public relations and media planning, are also the top firms in India. In 2016 they include Nielsen, Kantar (IMRB, HTA), IPSOS, IMS and GFR.

Market Research and Public Relations Functions

Market research in India is a good example, because it had taken roots because of insights and imagination of an Indian visionary, Vikram Sarabhai. ORG, founded by him, had become the fountainhead in no time and by 1975 it was a training ground for many other local agencies. Soon, the Indian Institutes of Managements were inspired to take on market research as an option for specialisation. But, with the government opening up the sector for foreign direct investments in 1991, no top market research agency remained Indian.

Of top ten market research firms dominating the Indian market in 2017, only two were there even earlier. Only a couple of firms retained their original name even after acquisition.

Table 21: Top 11 MR Firms

1.	Nielsen	7.	Hansa
2.	IMRB	8.	TNS
3.	IPSOS	9.	RNB Research
4.	IDC	10.	Data Matrix
5.	MRAS	11.	Millward Brown
6.	Iresearch Service		

The first Indian outfit, Operations Research Group (ORG) which pioneered market, media and opinion research over 30 years was taken over by Nielsen more than 20 years ago. MARG, the other Indian agency with impressive contribution, disappeared with Nielsen take over. Other agencies like Hansa, Mode, MRAS too changed hands, but retained the names. Today most of these are controlled by a multinational market research corporation, having direct or indirect association with a rating agency.

Public Relations Corporates

The function which advertising agencies were doing earlier has been carved out by the same agencies or one or other connected agencies of media or advertising as a profit-centre PR agency. These agencies or their functionaries operate in close collaboration with one or more market research and advertising agencies. They continue to play impressive role in building up ratings in general as well as in specific campaign contexts.

Table 22: Top Public Relations Companies in India

1.	Genesis Burson Marsteller
2.	Perfect Relations
3.	Wagner Shandwick
4.	Edelman

This activity continues to be dominated by individual companies. But these individuals are those companies who have close links with either a foreign advertising or market research company or to journalism and with media links or associations. In today's India, with about a thousand schools of all kind offering courses in public relations, there are as many public relations people who are journalists, many of them are freelancers, operating individually and under different nomenclature. Planting positive stories are the done thing today in media practices.

Media Agencies or Media Planning Corporates

They deal with space and time in media and decide about tariff and the kind of priority different newspapers or channels get at different points. They devise space/time packages and long-term contacts for placing commercials. They work in close association and coordination with rating agencies and use ratings to justify their priorities and tariff packages from time to time.

Table 23: Top Media Planning Agencies

1.	Mindshare	6.	Starcom Mediavest
2.	Madison Media	7.	OMD
3.	Nexus	8.	Allied Media
4.	Lodestar UM	9.	DDB Mudra Max
5.	Zenith Optimedia	10.	Group M

It was another turning point for Indian television, particularly the decade of 1993-2003, when with allowing of hundred per cent foreign direct investment in advertising, market research, public relations and media planning, they became mostly foreign controlled. Their principals were the same or linked or had common interests. The *TRP idea being a common interest service*, the four support services deepened penetration of ratings and build them as benchmark or yardstick. One cannot understand the phenomena of ratings and the kind of influence they yielded on the channels and their contents without understanding the origins and linkages between these various support services.

Group M is a leading media buying agency. It is part of the Kantar media research group, and is a 50 per cent partner of TAM media research. The fact that a significant share of television advertising outlays in the country is channelled through associates of Group M indicates the kind of link (or grip), that it has together with Nielsen on the TRP system. No wonder Group M has been an outright promoter of TAM. Its senior functionary in India, CV Srinivasan, for example, cautioned that if rating by TAM was not allowed, 'there would be no data, and TV ad spends could get impacted' and that such a 'situation is detrimental to the industry'. Srinivasan was quoted in *Business India,* justifying Kantar's appeal in the Delhi High Court in February 2014 against disqualification of TAM's rating operations.[17]

The Origins of Ratings

IT IS a mystery how TRPs came into common parlance and soon became a political jargon even in the Parliament and for the housewife in a remotely located household. TRP has been in the headlines of newspapers across the country for two decades. If it was not promoted deliberately and seriously, TRP would not have acquired such significance and prominence that it did within a span of the first five years. But now, in the last couple of years, TRP is often used to mean the opposite or to heckle or denigrate a public position. Consider for example: Rahul Gandhi, leader of the Congress party which ruled India for some decades, has accused the Prime Minister of playing 'TRP politics'. What does he mean? This was a three column headline in a serious daily, *The Economic Times*.[1] The context, the newspaper said, was that Rahul Gandhi meant that the Prime Minister was bluffing people or exaggerating affairs or misinterpreting realities on the ground. The term TRP clearly had acquired a negative connotation by 2010, especially used politically since 2014.

As if to revise such a sentiment, TAM surprisingly tried to replace TRP with TVT (television viewership in thousands) rather than as *per cent of audience share.* But that was too late to change TRP's negative usage. However, by then, the Broadcasting Audience Research Council had already progressed in its negotiation with TAM, fully owned by AC Neilsen and Kantar media of USA.

It is necessary to understand how TAM scuttled the idea of an independent BARC as suggested by TRAI and the Amit Mitra Committee way back in 2010. As half partner of AC Neilsen, Kantar even filed a case against BARC in Delhi High Court in January 2014.[2]

In the wake of the TRAI report and that of the Mitra[3] Committee on rating agencies, the government went ahead and issued a landmark notification on 16 January 2014, regulating rating activity in India. This notification ended TAM's regime. This initiative to regulate television rating was fifteen years too late and too little. Nevertheless, it finally made it obligatory for everyone engaged in rating television contents to register with the government of India (its authorised regulator) and the TRAI said, all such agencies had to fulfil certain conditions. The important ones were to do with *control* and *conflict of interest* aspects. It prescribed that 'no single entity engaged in ratings can hold paid up equity excess of 10 per cent simultaneously in a rating agency and broadcaster, and advertiser or advertising agency'.[4] It also indicated a minimum sample size of 20,000 panel homes reaching 50,000 people and scaling up in a couple of years. In a supportive step, the Delhi High Court even refused to stay the execution of that government notification regulating rating agency operations and cross media holdings. This meant disqualification of TAM from continuing to provide television rating as a service. And this in turn meant, clearing the functioning of BARC as the new rating agency.

However, like all government-inspired institutions, BARC could come up with its viewership report only by the end of 2015. That too, only after BARC had come to terms with TAM for a joint venture during mid-2015. *The joint venture is supposedly for 'meter management'.*

A close look at the joint agreement or understanding between the two (BARC and TAM) indicates that the agreement was about 'joint clients' and as promoter of the new business house, the Meteorology Data Private Ltd (MDL). TAM still continues (TAM 49% and BARC 51%) to provide its 'expertise' in India and continues 'to focus its efforts towards value adding....'

What does this mean? Two things are obvious in this understanding between BARC and TAM. First, *there is clear violation of not only 'in spirit' but 'on eligibility' criteria for a rating agency as per TRAI guidelines.* Second, *TAM retains its interest and 'hold on' rating operations in the country without accountability.* In fact, the arrangement with BARC has allowed TAM to now continue to offer certain (other) services to channels more formally (like advice on structure and scope of programmes, which it was offering informally). (However, BARC CEO Partho Dasgupta, in a 17 November 2017 meeting with me denied any such understanding with TAM and insisted that TAM had any role in its operations.)

To understand the mystery of how TRP has become the 'currency' for television industry in India, an analysis of happenings first for 1991-1994 period and then for 1994-1999 period gives us a better perspective than an analysis for the 1995-2015 period.

When ORG initiated television research from the 1970s, up until the 1990s, it was not with a meter or for any particular programmes. It was to find *which particular programme* or theme was recalled as 'viewed', remembered as 'seen' and what 'it meant' or how viewers related to what they had seen with their own attitudes and experiences. There was no pretension of sample being representative of various socio-economic sections of viewers.

The enquiry in that pre-TRP pursuit (of ORG, IMRB and even MARG) included why someone had 'not seen' a particular programme even when there was access to television. There was a lull period at ORG once the chief changed from Bhaskara Rao to Ashok Advani of *Business India,* under mysterious circumstances. Advani, thereafter, also took control of the other market research outfit, MARG, which was also trying to do field studies on television with Tito Ahluwalia as its chief.

It was at this point that AC Nielsen entered the Indian scene by taking over Advani's control of the premier Indian rating agencies, ORG and MARG. For them, the quickest service that could be offered in India and quickly emerge on the Indian stage was tracking and rating television viewing. And since they were operating a 'meter' for rating television viewership in a few other countries by then, they geared up ORG-MARG to take on and replicate the service in India despite the fact that the viewing scenario in Indian households and the kind of television sets and their spread at that time were not exactly compatible for such meter-based capture of viewership with reliability.

Thus 200 to 400 meters (removed for updating in South Africa) were initially imported, presumably to experiment in India under the ORG-MARG-INTAM banner. Since this meter was primarily to ascertain whether the television set was just 'on', it had no provision to take into account the family as a unit. Initially, a CD with data was collected weekly from each of those selected television-owning households by a ORG-MARG field researcher, where the meter was installed, of course, with the consent of the household.

It was after one year that, what is called a 'people meter', was brought in and the earlier meters were replaced (1994).

This 'people meter' had buttons for every member of the household (up to 10). This meant that, a TV set 'being on' in a house with a meter fitted did not mean everyone in the house were in front of the TV and were actually viewing what was available on that particular TV screen for a reasonable duration. Viewership, as recorded on CD or on-line, could only be a *deduction* of viewership. *It was just a switching on and off record, not of how many in a household watched which particular programme.*

The system of arriving at viewership adopted in the 'people meter' project gets complicated as more and more elements are added to the survey and, in that process, both relevance and reliability of data gets questioned. With the 'people meter', every member of the family above four years of age (and now, of over two years of age) is expected to be active and take to viewing as an 'assignment'—that is push the on button on the meter or (somewhat like the TV remote) the assigned button (one for each individual member of a household) only, and also the off button on the same meter, each time s/he goes out of viewing range of the television set. That was the time when Murdoch took control of Star TV in India.

The marketing model followed by Nielsen was: first enlist as subscribers and supporters, from among multinational marketing corporations in India who were the major advertisers at the time and advertising agencies (who discriminate one media from another and one channel and the other for placing advertisements and allocating ad outlays). Overseas principles of those advertisers and ad agencies were already by then customers of Nielsen's marketing services (and it suited them to engage the same agency for its services in India as well). This was what happened initially. In any case, Nielsen also used advertising to promote its rating services in India distinctly.

Third, the new public relations corporates who had just entered India were involved in getting special media coverage for Nielsen and its media ratings.

Fourth, cross channel promotion of ratings helped to speed up the process and get bandwagon advantage. How else, for example, does Colors channel get rated high within the first couple of weeks of its launch in India?

Fifth, glamour and glitter in the serials is ensured, as in the case of Star group's channels, as special identity (apart from other content strategies that ratings promoted and Star chose to feature on Star TV). Together, these thrusts helped TRPs in a big way.

The PR had ensured that TRP figures become news stories

for prominent coverage. Once on comfortable course in that regard, TAM was registered as a separate company in 1998 to take on formally TRP as its own 'brand' ambassador and as the currency of advertising and media business. The next step was drop ORG-MARG tags for its own TAM identity and standing.

Is Popularity and TRP the Same?

Popularity is an outcome of strategies.

Public relation professionals can convert a novelty into a popularity, build or showcase an exception into a generality, and create band-wagoning. Anything new attracts curiosity and also attention. But making everything or every time a 'news' is PR. Novelty effect is well known. But channelling it for a larger scheme of things is what results in TRP becoming a benchmark. Any such attribute stands to advantage even in recall methodology and thereafter, if the programme stands out and is accessible, it could cause the necessary push to the push-on button, particularly when the programme is produced with glamour and glitter and suspense or interactively, and spark emotions of women and children. For example, viewership of a continually telecast programme like *Friends* (first aired in 2004). It is still being shown by channels. Those who want to see it, tune in to that particular channel. Then, of course, anything specially promoted and marketed for long, will accrue special advantage. In this process, foreign, curiosity or suspense and emotionalised television content gets extra attention, like adventure runs. This was what got reflected in the ratings, based on meter-centric instant or momentary responses of a few urban TV-owning householders.

Is the rating for channels or programmes or for both? To start with, programmes of Star TV were made to stand out distinctly. The foundation for this channel was made so formidable that popularity of the channel and most of its programmes gained special advantage. All those ratings were with only around 500 metered TV households initially in Mumbai and Delhi, and another 9 cities added for coverage with (1200) meters in the next one year. And yet, ratings were presented as if they were spread in entire urban India or the readings were for the country.

Then the inherent limitations of trying to measure week after week with same (mostly) size of the sample and same specific pre-identified families became obvious to promoters. In the early 1990s, when video and satellite connectivity was just catching up and transition or migration from terrestrial to cable connectivity and from cable to satellite happened fast, (more recently to digital), certain fallacy in comparative assessment (which is what the advertising community needs) were obvious in television ratings. For example, viewing situations and viewing options are not 'uniform'. Nielsen chose to ignore the obvious, probably because no one in India, especially the government, did not question it. Channels were added constantly as new programmes/serials were and new TV-owning households were added constantly throughout the decade, throughout the country. This data is constantly changing even now, as India is still only a developing country and not a developed country.

One needs to know if the sample is 'television households' as a unit, against when the sample was disaggregated and also of individuals in a household. When sample comprises only 'satellite TV households', that data has to be presented accordingly (or the public told, that was how the data was derived). This data cannot be put across as data of all households nationally. The ratings were not sensitive of such rapid changes and shifts in the television scenario in the country.

The situation in this regard was totally different in 1991-95, in terms of connection source and channel options available and also in the mode of opting or change in viewing pattern, with channel remote control in hand as against the fixed meter recorder in the house where television was located at a fixed place in the house. The figures of the rating agency did not distinctly indicate the base for estimating viewers for different segments of TV households.

An analysis of ratings for some sampled weeks between 2000 and 2008 indicates the fallacy. For 15 weeks, the order of programmes rated were analysed. Most, or all households, covered were of cable and satellite households. In the rating for nine of fifteen weeks, all top ten programmes were of Star TV. Only in three weeks, there was one programme of Doordarshan in the top ten and all three were of cricket matches. Just five or six were of Zee TV, 2 or 3 were of Sony, and one programme was of Color TV.

What were these programmes and what were DD programmes during the period that ranked in the weekly top ten? Of 18 programmes of Star TV that were shown as on the top ten rankings between 2000 and 2008 week after week, more than half of them were produced by Balaji (in which Star TV was a key share holder at the time) Studios. Three Doordarshan programmes shown on the top in November 2007, were cricket matches, where Doordarshan had telecasting rights as the national channel. This analysis brings out that ratings made available to the public were of cable and satellite households. Secondly, that no programme in news and current affairs category were viewed to rank on the top ten, going by these TAM ratings for 2000-2008 period.

In the October-December 2005 issue of *Vidura* magazine of Press Institute of India, Vidya Sahai wrote about the 'Myths and realities of TV Ratings'.[5] The first para of that lead article is reproduced here for its cryptic way of summing up about TRPs at that time, reflecting a view outside of the advertising community. 'It was Friday. The top TV news channels were offering prayers – some for favourable TV Rating Points (TRP) and a few others for the position number one. And it worked for Star News. The TRP that fateful Friday shattered the habitual perception of invincibility of the *Sabse Tez* news channel – Aaj Tak – when the Smartest channel – Star News – overtook them in their weekly race for number one. The villain of the piece was TV Audience Media (TAM) research.'

This analyse shows first, how TRPs were anxiously awaited by channels (not advertisers) week after week; second, how the position in the ranking based on TRPs was critical for advertising tariff; and, thirdly, how Star News Channel outsmarted or overtook the other competitive channels. This article in 2005 was one of the earliest to appear, signalling certain oddness about top ten rankings projected and promoted by way of TRPs.

The period of 1994-95 – 1998-99 was one of expansion and consolidation for channels. With the number of channels multiplying, particularly of the Star TV group, the meter-based INTAM rating service acquired wheels and got consolidated.

The rating service was offered initially in the name of ORG - MARG although both the organisations were already part of AC Nielsen. Significance of this period was that with unleashing of TRPs, new channels which at that point meant Star, Zee and Sony, got a leap in their viewership, leaving behind the channels like Doordarshan which had been there for some years but suffered from certain monotony effects, mostly due to poor technical quality, fewer or no programme options and no programme promotion, and lacked suspense and surprises that a 24-hour visual media offers. Also, programmes of regional channels during those early years did not get their position reflected in the TRPs.

An analysis of Doordarshan during the decade 1984-1995 brings out that its performance on the programme front was not as disappointing as was made out to be and propagated to be via TRPs and its PR. It suited the rating agency to show that DD was not good enough in order to make its foray into India, as the new channels at that time, primarily of cable and satellite origin were limited at that time to few urban clusters and the rating agency covered primarily those very city clusters.

Starting with *Humlog* (1984), *Buniyad* (1986-87), *Ramayana-Mahabharata* (1987-90) and *Chitrahar*, *Superhit Muquabala*, *Shaktiman* (1998-05) etc. DD, during this decade, had beefed up its programming. But that never got reflected as viewership meters were set up selectively in satellite TV households. Noticeably, even Ekta Kapoor of Balaji Telefilms started with Doordarshan with *Kayamat*, *Ithiaas* and like programmes and then with Zee TV before moving to Star TV and hitting the rating bonanza.

With such a range of programmes, *Doordarshan had a*

network and reach which no new satellite channel had at that time. But Doordarshan never took to public communication and remained low profile and, in fact, lacked analyses and futures perspective, and a master to guide it. *A critical analysis indicates that Doordarshan suffered more because of Prasar Bharati and the Ministry. They deprived it breath to catch up with the fast-changing television scenario.* Such a lapse at Doordarshan came handy for the rating agency to push forward with what suited its own consolidation and expansion plans and become some kind of a new 'power centre' and an 'ally of foreign channels'.

DART, a weekly assessment of television viewership by Doordarshan's own Audience Research,[6] was based on personal interviews with TV households using recall method but eliciting far more insights, and for viewer end status. *DART was neither given a fair chance nor made to continue for a while to gain the ground needed for acceptability from other channels as well.* And audience research officers become demoralised with Doordarshan too subscribing to INTAM/TAM ratings, and taking weekly TRPs seriously.

In this process of quick transition, rating by INTAM/TAM did not go through the kind of scrutiny required before scaling up. This is particularly because that was the time when the strategically so-called 'people meter' got away with its limitations without even key stakeholders knowing what it was all about and its reliability. No one raised the kind of minimum questions that one should before taking something as a criteria or basis and pay heavy amount as subscription. This is partly because the advertising community had already gone ahead and endorsed the idea and accepted the agency (AC Nielsen) involved without posing any such basic questions.

All this helped consolidation of Nielsen on the scene directly and that was how TAM was officially registered in 1998.

The kind of promotion and build-up for *Kaun Banega Crorepati* had come handy both for the rating agency and, of course, for the Star channels. The next step to consolidate and tighten the grip of ratings was merger of TAM and INTAM (2001) to become one currency of the industry. Although the merger was because of global player WPPs take-over of Nielsen and increasing discrepancies in the two ratings, an impression was spread that the merger was 'to service the advertising industry and channels better'. It was a compulsion turned into a strategy.

Against such a backdrop, was it a surprise that by 2000, week after week it was Star TV's 'family serials' that got rated on the top – as if the ratings were of only Star channels 'not of all TV channels' as they were said to be? In fact, for many weeks for the next six or seven years, more of top ten rated programmes were of Star TV. Only in a few weeks did feature programmes of Zee TV and Sony get to the top ten.

Since neither INTAM nor TAM covered India initially, there wasn't any estimate for viewership of any of Doordarshan channels or its specific programmes as *reach* of those channels were spread across the country, unlike most other channels. However, viewership for the *Ramayana* and *Mahabharata* serials was estimated on an adhoc basis by the news media to be around 100 million. And yet, even they were not on the top, not even in the top ten rated programmes by TAM/INTAM.

Curiously, viewership apart, there were efforts on the part of satellite channels, Star and Sony in particular, to acquire some serials that ran on Doordarshan channels earlier. In fact, there were more than half a dozen old serials of Doordarshan during this period (1990–2000), which were rerun on some other channel including Star and Sony. *Buniyad* is one example. Many others, like for example *Bharat Ek Khoj* of Shyam Benegal, could not be acquired by Star because of the copyright.

Then there was some 'type' of serials popular on Doordarshan which the new foreign-controlled channels did not emulate. And the rating agency, for curious reason, never reflected the popularity of 'that kind of' programmes in its ratings. One specific example is *Rajini* (and another is *Nukkad*), a Sunday reality-type programme, when reality genre had not become part of the menu of satellite channels.

Why? Of course, the rating agency had not yet taken off with TRP. Why such genre was never allowed to be assessed reflects the motive of TRPs. Mudra Advertising agency, which sponsored *Rajini* was made to withdraw (I was present in a discussion with AG Krishna Murthy, CEO of Mudra in Ahmadabad, on one Sunday morning while watching *Rajini* when he told me about the kind of pressures he was being subjected to, to withdraw the sponsorship).[7]

My understanding then was that it was targeted for death, as *Rajini* was crusading for consumer activism and fighting against consumerism. The serial was not only dropped by sponsors, but intriguingly never was there a *Rajini*-type serial thereafter! (Other examples include *Nukkad* and *Udaan* serials.) Why such 'successful' serials on Doordarshan were not allowed to be supported for the next few years is no great mystery. Ekta Kapoor, whose serials were on Doordarshan, on the other hand, was inducted and oriented to produce 'certain kind' of 'K-series serials' as per the Star group's vision for India. Themes Star propagated soon became the parameter for regional language channels.

Uday Shankar,[8] CEO of Star TV then, stands out as an exception who experimented with new approach, ideas, formats and schedules, even departing from the limited outlook of channels otherwise. As a visionary, he even tried out with programmes like *Kaun Banega Crorepati* with Amitabh Bachchan, *Satyamev Jayate* with Amir Khan. Equally important, Shankar continues to articulate innovative outlook for channels and condemns the recent retrograde trends in media in India. Shankar stands out as a Star for the best of media in India.

The period of 1995-2001 was one of conversion of ratings into some kind of mania across the board, as if that was all that mattered, and all channels including Doordarshan fell in line and went in for weekly ratings of TAM. The beneficiary was Star TV and Sony and their affiliates. The biggest loser was Doordarshan.

The advertising community cannot be blamed for such a fall for Doordarshan. A retrospective analysis brings out how successive Union governments remained mute all through. Even more, the civil society, particularly the academic faculties, remained unconcerned about the kind of programme priorities that were hyped and recycled. Apart from CMS, only certain women's groups, mostly of the CPI and CPM, took up the matter, condemning the rating criteria. They also voiced their displeasure in the Parliament.

What is TRP All About?

What is TRP? Television Rating Point (TRP) has been much used (or is it misused) and is a maligned concept. Over the last two decades, it has become a jargon and lingo and a yardstick to describe the state of affairs of television, its priorities and concerns at a macro level as well as at a micro (channel) level. TRP reflects standing of a channel and individual programme or a time-segment of a channel, in a relative context as recorded by a specially devised meter attached to a television set/screen in a selected few television-owning households.

TRP is based on whether a television set (or other device that could play) in preselected and metered TV households, is 'on' or 'off' and a pushbutton record of who in that household has pushed the button on the meter.

A commercially operated rating agency claimed this function as 'viewing' of a television screen, although that may not necessarily or actually be so in some households or at some times and contexts. Although the TV may have been on, no one may be there in front of the screen, or in and out, as that depends on the layout of typical household where the television set is positioned in the household and also the family habits (eat together, watch together, where asleep etc.).

Also, meter installation in a TV household assumes or implies that the household has agreed or consented or volunteered to operate the meter while proceeding to watch television, whatever channel or programme interests them. This, of course, assumes that the television set has options available technically for all networks or channel packages. (That also depends on the way the subscription packages are promoted by DTH or MSOs and local cable operator.) The meter is attached only to such television-owning households where the TV set has such options technically. Obviously, households with 'older television' sets are not in the sample. Also, it is not known or disclosed as to what number of households considered for a week for assessment were of cable connection only or satellite connection.

There is another aspect, which is to do with human behaviour or the kind of role that each member of the household who is expected to switch off and on plays. This means, while in the first instance when the TV set is being switched on, it does not necessarily mean the person in the radius of the TV screen is looking at a programme on television. For, *looking at* television may not necessarily mean *viewing* what is on the screen every time and all the time although that could be assumed.

Recall your own experience! This is particularly in the case of children of less than 7 years, who were part of the coverage of 'viewership' initially. These kids are expected to push on or off (or someone else around does that on their behalf) in this kind of meter reading. Even a two-year-old in the household is taken in as sample in this kind of analysis. That can only be surrogate. Was that ever indicated in the TRP result?

Have you ever thought out, why does a household agree or allow a meter to be set up on their TV set and also agree to operate it regularly and every time? And all the members of the household comply!

Such a meter consumes electricity, however marginal that may be and at first people believed that the meter, a gadget, has no threat of snooping, privacy etc. This element is taken care of by the rating agency by offering certain amount of money or gift to the household in return or in lieu of allowing the meter to function on a continuing basis. After that installation, which channel or which programme a household watches is their choice unless or otherwise they were also motivated directly or indirectly, either by the same agency which had set up the meter or by someone else who knew about the meter, to watch TV during certain times and watch a certain channel or programme or watch for a certain duration or/and by certain members of the household (children, women, young etc.).

Then came 'people meter' in 1998. That is, the earlier meter on the set top box was upgraded or replaced with another one having a special panel (remote or otherwise) with up to nine buttons to switch on and off by each member of the household. Now, the process was: each time a member of the family or household starts looking at the television screen when it is on, he or she in the household is to push a particular button allocated so that particular person's viewership is recorded by the meter fixed on the set top. This he or she is expected to do even though watching a programme selected ahead, by a predecessor or another member of the family who had already pushed the button allocated to him or her. This panel is equipped with a button for every member in the family or household and also provided a button for a visitor (the phenomena of visitors from neighbourhood to a TV-owning household was significant in the earlier decade), depending on where the household was located. A switch is assigned to the old and young in the household and each is expected to push only that button assigned, each and every time he or she starts looking or watching the television screen and switch 'off' that particular button only when going out of the viewing range of television in the household. All that requires certain deliberate consciousness and deliberate discipline on the part of every member in the household and every time. Knowing Indian households, this is a naturally improbable expectation, no matter what the incentive. Any student of psychology will tell you, such a reading has no probability of accuracy. *Imagine how the political and technical authorities in India were made a fool of, how the watchdogs academia and media failed the people even as a new century began.*

From out of this process or pattern of meter recording of 'on' and 'off' was deduced the 'viewership' not only for television in general but in particular for channels and programme or time chunks as this meter was already fitted with such information and capabilities to automatically identify the channel and also the programme on screen at that time.

The agency had provision to include or delete or rearrange each time and every time a new channel was added or a programme feature is added or deleted by a channel so that when a button connected to the meter is pushed, the correct channel or correct programme being telecast at that time is recorded.

This had to change when channels proliferated so much and so frequently, and programmes too were changed or added with and without notice so frequently. In the 'people meter' process, the central computer centre of the meter provider is expected to update as often. Today, this update matching is done by BARC with channel-wise programme data supplied by TAM. In 2000, BARC did not exist, it was just TAM. The technicality of such capability for a meter has not been questioned here. The human interface aspect, convenience and discipline aspect of each viewer in the household has been. Also, can such 'mechanical function' be considered as 'viewing behaviour'?

The process of doing this on-off operation over time/weeks could, of course, only be presumed as 'change' in the 'behaviour'.

There is no 'measurement' otherwise involved in this process of coming up with figures for viewership. At the analysis stage, there could be quantification of frequency of looking at the TV screen and the programme on that channel at that time.

How many have ever seen such a meter or know of a household having such a meter? Over the years (2000-2010), this has been a question I posed to whomever I met in conferences in Delhi and outside and all those meetings I attended to discuss viewership. I am yet to find one person who has seen such a 'people meter' in operation or otherwise! Even more surprising, I have asked around and none of the advertiser or the ad agency executives had seen such a meter before accepting the viewership figures at the outset, I was told.

This may be because TAM, the operating agency, never wanted people to know how cumbersome the meter was and there was no transparency in going about with the meter. In any case, they were set up in insignificant number of households. The invisibility was perhaps also because this meter arrangement was supposed to be confidential as TAM did not want to disclose which household had such a meter (and may be, even the agency apprehended certain opposition to the very idea of a meter and its architecture for different reasons). No wonder, Krishnan of TAM did not bring a meter on 7 March 2007 to the CMS round table at India International Centre, New Delhi, despite a specific request.

Rating: When channels and programmes are arranged by a sequence, as per data derived from the meter as described above, the list is considered as 'ranking'. And 'rating' is viewed as per cent or share of total viewing.

Also 'viewership' is something a channel or a programme

maintains over time. This *over time* factor could be over twenty-four hours or one week or a month etc.

'Point' refers to relative weightage as per viewing recorded by the meter in the total viewing time of the period in context (week or month or daily). Based on such 'measurement' of channels or programmes in a relative context and over a given time period, points are derived.

When is a person considered as a 'viewer'? If the button of an individual is on for one minute in a day, would that person be considered as a viewer or should that be five minutes in a time segment? Or, let us ask what is the cut-off point? This could be different from an advertiser's point of view and that of a feature programme's or news channel's or news bulletin's point of view or of one-day cricket coverage's.

One issue is regarding frequency of reporting. TAM issued weekly ratings. When I-map[9] came, it talked of on-line ratings but issued daily ratings. But the News Broadcast Association suggested (in 2012) that TAM should issue monthly reports instead of weekly. However, this suggestion was resisted by advertisers and advertising agencies. The meter is equipped to transmit data to a central server every night. Some channels like Colors advocated daily reports with rating data.

The question is not one of determining revenues generated from rating service but of reliability and consistency in data (not uniformity across). The other fundamental issue is the misleading aspect of ratings when they are daily or on-line.

Television Advertisement Measurement Private Limited, the company which had introduced, promoted and popularised TRP as its commercial brand, is popularly known as TAM. It also offers five or six other services to do with media contents and schedules using different brand names, all to do with media operations. Some of them involve conflict of interest with its TRP service. *What had started as a support service for advertising industry has become a content and programme determiner or a guiding measure for channel viability in India.*

BARC is now using the term 'impression' in place of 'viewer'.

TRP is totally a quantitative exercise. It does not have any characteristics of qualitative dimensions. It, however, indicates a 'trend' over time and from that, one can deduct or draw upon certain observations on the 'why' aspect involved in availing options on a television set.

Since TRP is a quantitative exercise, arrived in a relative context, the figures and percentages cannot be considered uniformly reliable and used in isolation or in a stand-alone manner, particularly for content priorities, programme strategies and creative options. True, quantitative trend makes better sense and gives insights when integrated with experiences and observations in a qualitative context and on qualitative dimensions. *However, 'margin of error' aspect in that process cannot be uniform for all segments of households or for all categories of programmes or genres.* Is this indicated anytime in presenting TAM figures? This margin of error in TRPs could be anywhere between 25 per cent to 60 per cent, depending upon location, socio-economics segment of the household and whether it is viewership among children and differs from news channels to sports channel to science channel.

The TRP system has gone through several bad patches, '*badnam*', from time to time in the last decade as many programmes of some channels and the priorities of television itself have come under criticism for irrelevance and blatant deviation from societal and cultural values in India. Yet, such programmes were indicated as of 'high viewer preference' under the TRP system and prompted a copycatting phenomenon to the extent of influencing creative talents of writers and producers. This was possible because of the inane or irrelevant or both system of capturing the on and off aspect, using a remote of a meter. The kind of mismatch or allegations of manipulation that the meter system has gone through and the way the outcome of rating procedure was popularised and perpetuated by channels and advertisers has always been suspect.

People Meter or Family Meter?

When the Electronic Voting Machine (EVM) was introduced on an experimental basis (1988 and for entire country in 2004), its reliability was questioned, and complaints were lodged. In fact, doubts about tampering and manipulation of EVM continues even in 2018 and the Election Commission of India (ECI) has had to have rounds of meetings with political parties and activists and has even appointed an experts' group (Professor PV Indiresan, Former Director of IIT) to look into public apprehensions. This was even after voters had experienced the using of the EVM in more than one election. ECIL, Hyderabad, was the one which had designed and continue to manufacture EVMs (even exports to other countries) and ECI has been using these EVMs for general elections all over India since 2004. But, even after two decades, every time there is an election, the ECI publicly demonstrates EVMs and educates voters on how they can vote, using an EVM. Even in Assembly elections in 2017, the ECI repeated such an exercise.[11]

After more than a year of using (1991-93) a meter for capturing television viewership to make people believe that such and such a programme of x or y channel was being viewed by xyz per cent of the total population, public were told that INTAM and (later) TAM were using state-of-art technology in this 'meter' (and in the people meter later) to monitor on and off of persons in selected TV households where such a meter was fixed.

Beyond that, nothing was told to any one formally as to what this meter was all about, its origin and how it works and what it indicates or records and what maintenance it requires and what kind of tampering is possible. Not even a photograph of any meter was ever in the public domain or media, nor was there ever any demonstration anywhere about any effort to sensitise the opinion making public about the functioning of the meter or of its reliability. It is not rocket science, a meter is a piece of technology, not a national secret.

In reality, the sample of TV owning households selected for installing the meter was so small (less than a couple of thousand at that time) that no one had a chance even to get to know about these meters. And yet, the figures put out to the public through the news media week after week were as if they were national, reliable, reflective, revealing, comprehensive and inclusive of everyone in the household (even of visitor and the domestic help!).

By 1993, this secretive TRP data was already being publicised widely and used by advertising agencies as the basis for spending thousands of crores of rupees. Channels too started to reorient their content strategies and programme priorities, based on this TRP data. By the time questions on the relevance and authenticity of TRP was raised, the stakeholders and the country had already taken to TRPs as the criteria for media budgets, advertising strategies and even for programme strategies by channels. And, even more tellingly, for determining ad tariff. Would that have been possible without serious and strategic reinforcement efforts by key players? And in that process TV viewers in the country were taken to a band-wagoning phenomenon!

Since BARC is also using the *same meters* (except that it proposes to get these meters made in India at a much less cost), we should get to know more about this (people) meter or whatever it is (Bar-o-Meter) BARC is calling the meter now.

How does a 'people meter' work? The architecture of meter includes display unit, remote control, basic unit, transmission unit connecting to central server located somewhere else every night. Unlike the earlier first meter, 'people meter' (or Bar-o-Meter of BARC) has a panel, with up to nine buttons earmarked for each member of the family, plus buttons on the same panel for a helper at home and for visitors (up to two) to the household. Each such member who has been assigned a button on the panel is expected to push 'on' that button on that panel on coming into viewing range of a TV set and, equally importantly, push the 'off' button of the same panel while going out of the range of the TV set or stop looking at the TV. Imagine people doing this in a working and busy household. Have you seen anyone you know or heard of any household using such a meter?

Even in 21st century and hi-tech India, we are supposed to accept and believe that this on-off act is 'viewing' (now by BARC) whichever content is telecast at a time point on the TV and during the period and that this will tell us about the popularity of a channel or programme. With the TV-remote becoming a handy operating tool, the viewing meter is supposed to be driven to record the exact duration of the time during which a particular member in the household is in a viewing range.

At whose instance or on whose preference in the family, at that time point, was a particular programme being watched (who pushed the ON button first) is not clear in this kind of rating. This implies that not all those who come under the 'viewing radius' is an 'active viewer'. Some could be 'passive viewer' and another could be a 'casual viewer', not all of them could be lumped in the same category of 'viewers'. And then, of course, is the concern whether that viewing act of a member is just a 'glance' of less than a minute or five minutes. Why is the distinction between 'active viewer', 'casual viewer' and 'passive viewer' not considered? Is this not important and pertinent? Is *looking at* and '*watching*' same?

Compatibility of this meter with the model of the television set in a household sampled for the purpose could also be a limiting factor for the reliability of the meter attached (otherwise it amounts to limiting to households having sets purchased in the recent years, or the latest model).

In a typical situation, in one TV-owning household, one can say that what is recorded as is being 'viewed' by such a meter is what the 'family views' (not anyone in particular or any particular member of the family), because the choice or preference of what exactly is being viewed and when exactly it is viewed is decided by one member of the family or by some members together. For example, a family with children will only switch on and see children's channels and this is decided by the parent. Some child may not watch the programme at all even if the set is on, while a second child may. This in no way provides assessment of a programme's preference by parents as they may not be viewers. At the same time, it may provide parent preference for the kids, without the parents watching. As such, a 'people meter' is more a 'family meter' and most of the time this is the same as the earlier meter, with only one button on the panel for on and off, unless the household has more than one TV set.

BARC has claimed that 5 per cent of its sampled household has more than one TV set working in the house.[12] But the agency claims, its sample consists of everyone individually in the family of 4 years plus (husband, wife and children). That is, if the number of meters installed is 3000 in TV-owning households, the sample is only 3000, not 3000 multiplied by the number of above 4-year-old members in the family, which would make it between 9,000 to 12,000. Perhaps it was for this reason that BARC included two-year-olds too instead of limiting its assessment to 4-year-old.

However, in 2013, TAM claimed its sample was over 30,000 households. Not all members in a household can be considered as viewers every time. As such, figures put out in a dis-aggregated way could not have been accurate every time and every week. The reliability of viewership, given at any point, may be better at the household level, but, reliability of age 2 to 4 and 4 to 9 is unlikely to be the same as of other ages. Similarly, in the case of certain socio-economic sections in the sample, the reliability could be altogether different. That is why, the margin of error could be widely different in each case. This, of course, also depends on the extent of viewing in the household or of certain category of members from week to week.

Given the kind of structure and layout of most houses even in cities, the chances of pushing the *on* and *off* button each time by each member of the family coming in front of the television set and going out of range by each member is likely to be significantly different. Whatever be the kind of briefing given to the members of the household by the rating agency which sets up the meter, meticulous observance/obedience cannot be expected, especially in the Indian context and no one can claim to stable readings over a period of time. Also it matters where the meter (different from the TV remote) is kept – is it on the television set itself or is someone holding it or is it kept in the middle of the room or in a corner, within the radius of the television set or away from it.

In the case of some households, this promptness and accuracy of pushing on or off depends on what kind of 'incentive' is offered by the agency to the household or members of the family, generally and specially. The complaints or allegations that were in circulation about meters a few years ago (and even more recently with BARC) was because of this susceptibility. That is—whether family members are given special incentives for watching at certain times or for certain duration or certain programmes. This is still not clear and not known. Whether any special incentive was offered by the agency which had set up the meter, or someone else who knew that such a meter was in operation in that house, had offered any special incentive is not also known. Since under the sampling plan, each metered TV owning household has certain weightage, it represents a few lakhs of TV households. Even a couple of metered TV households succumbing to such 'lures' at any point in time could vitiate the projected TRP numbers and the very ranking itself, thereby boosting prospects of some channels and harming some others.

This 'people meter' has led to more instances of compromise, or manipulation, and inaccuracy in the projections. This has happened more often by ranking as per a (pre) understanding with the channel, or with a particular programme producer. There were allegations earlier of some channels being 'pre-assured of TRPs'! (Refer to the round table on viewership at the Hyderabad-based CESS, a government supported institute.)

Moreover, this 'people meter' remains of the same architecture, although two decades of new technologies have come to capture viewing more *accurately* instead of *approximately* as it has been for all these years. BARC has not yet (in the tail end of 2018) put out the architecture of the meter it is getting made in India. It describes its meter just as a Bar-o-Meter, with a hand-held remote control for on and off by the members of the family. In 2017, BARC announced[13] an agreement with a French meter company for a state-of-the-art meter but without indicating its features. It is yet to be seen in what way this will improve accuracy of viewership estimates of TAM.

There are three fundamental issues here. First, to what extent the on-and-off of a button of a 'people meter' reflects *actual viewing* of 'spontaneous viewer'? Is it more of a potential viewership record or the result of a 'deduction exercise' or is it based on the assumption that everyone in front of a TV set is an actual 'viewer'.

Second, the very idea of instant tracking or on-line monitoring of viewing, using this meter is somewhat like concluding and also awarding who the winner is, based on any one set in a tennis match instead of waiting for all the sets of the match. That is misleading, both in the case of less-than-a-minute commercials and programmes of 30 minutes or more.

Third, the way the projections are made, claiming every four (and two) plus age group in the household as part of the sample, is a fallacy or a chance phenomenon. Then the question of whether the 'people meter' is for tracking by *looking at* a programme or a channel, or both, and, if so, with what reliability in each case?

The structure and scope of this process of viewership estimation is more to cater to the requirements of advertising which, often, gives more weightage for the *looked at* phenomena. But then, to what extent does this meter cater to or captures 15 or 25 or 35 seconds is doubtful, although the meter recording is expected to be a continuing one.

Then there are other issues like surrogating, where one member pushes the 'on or off' on behalf of another member of the family or even a visitor or helper. Initially it was claimed that the meter was 'measuring viewership'. Later, it was described as an exercise in recording of eye-balls. Now BARC is providing *impressions* in thousands. What difference has this made or is expected to make, only time can tell.

Once the TV owning households with a meter are known to the outside, the higher the chances of family members coming under inducement and the rating under manipulation. Can identity of TV households be kept secret, which even the TRAI expects? Even if it is possible, it could only be for a few months initially. It is a matter of time for the meter game[14] to multiply!

As long ago as in 1993, I had suggested changing a certain per cent of the total sample of metered TV households periodically with a new panel of TV households. It was much after that, that TAM claimed it was doing such a (after 2005) replacement of TV households. But by that time, TRP had come to stay.[15]

Limits of TRP

When we have a vast network of television stations and wide spread viewership, we should know who is viewing, when, how often and also what. We must also know what is the effect or influence of such viewing. For this, we should first know how many television sets are on and for how long and why there is fluctuations in their on and off buttons on the meters. But to know about *actual viewership* we need to establish relations between that set being on and someone actually watching. For that, *a different methodology is needed.* TRPs is not enough to capture both these phenomena.

By making TRP as the ultimate and an all-round criteria, the country has ignored the basics and what is known as the *effects research* altogether, particularly research on a programme's effect on children and in the context of social development issues. As a result, there was never a public debate on the contents of channels. Then, of course, there are also questions on the appropriateness of the meters being imported and its use with all or most television sets with a remote control for channel surfing that could be used even away from the viewer-meter. That such a meter is being used in USA or elsewhere to market 'viewership' should not and cannot be a compelling reason for Indian society to settle on *as it is*, yes *as it is* or *as is where is* basis.

How many such meters did TAM have in 2014 when BARC took over rating and with how many meter homes is still not actually known. TAM had less than 1000 meters in 1995 and it was 12,000 in 2013, it said.[10] Therefore, how TRP was made a common currency for television in India initially (between 1991-95) is a big story by itself.

Viewing Television and Cinema

An analysis of the themes and contents prioritised by cinema in India, before and after proliferation of competitive television and TRP, reveals marked change and variation in production values and content themes and subject priorities. Whether this change in themes was on account of TRP-led television or economic reforms and changed realities in the country or in what combination of all those is something that can be debated academically and there may not be uniformity in opinions.

Priorities in content themes of visual mass media (which earlier meant cinema) until the eighties was based mostly on concerns of the producer or/and director individually. What bothered them earlier were what featured in their films. It was mostly exploitation of, conflicts and conflict situations both social and economic (when they were not on mythological themes). What can be said about today's themes? For example, show masters of cinema had set good examples. Raj Kapur's cinemas were full of exploitation and conflicts, dilemma of socio-economic transition in the country. So also, emotional cinema man Bimol Roy's work, or even art film-maker Shantaram's productions. Neither of them denigrated fundamental and foundational values of India or compromised virtues unique to the country. Nor did those cinema pioneers promote greed in people (although pointed it out) as a superior virtue. On the contrary, there were efforts to show or depict *good* winning at the end.

The 'reality' they presented in cinema was far more stimulating than the 'reality shows' of television channels today. The competitiveness that cinema was engaged in was not 'at any cost' or 'by any means' or for immediate temporal gains. Nor were they based on denigrating relationships between people or trust in each other, nor did they threaten the simple living styles. And, long-term implications or influence of film was a concern of cinema producers unlike television channels today. Interestingly, the background of most of the film producers of previous decades was humble and they were from the grassroots and self-made individuals. In television on the other hand, both *bad* and *good* is shown in such a way that *bad* is easily emulated or adopted, as some studies of some television serials have indicated.

When it comes to television, it is more about *interesting people,* shown by whichever means! The idea of interesting people, luring people to see or attract them even casually or instantly, can easily be traced to television channels. How did it happen? Once it is a number game, that is, once the number of people looking at a screen is a sufficient criterion, that has become the basis for such a phenomena.

It is not so much change, effects, conflict resolution or problem solving or sensitising people that matter in such an evaluation. Going by motivating factors for such a phenomenon, TRP can be credited for the shift in *what matters* even in the case of the powerful television media. The notion of TRP has given wheels and wings to such evaluative criteria for the paradigm shift from *concerned cinema* to that of *no holds barred programmes*. Now, it is not a producer or a director who alone makes the content and course, as in cinema. In the case of television channels, because of high cost of production and promotion and compulsions for revenue collections, it is the channels that dictate the shows.

Cinema is also a 'commercial service', the same way or more so, just as television is. The difference is that in television, support or sponsorship is direct, whereas in the case of cinema it is tickets sold which is called the 'box office' collection, and access to cinema theatres that matter and determine success. *Cinema viewers are not captive as in the case of television. One has to plan to go to see a film, which is pre-censored by a designated government agency for violence and sex, offensive to sentiments of any section of people etc. Neither of these limits matters much in the case of television in India.* Television builds itself more often with suspense, from one episode to another. An individual film may many-a-times make a long-lasting impact. It is the 'sitcom' status of television and the cumulative impact of its contents that make the difference. It is gratification at the click of a remote button, it can come in doses, at a specified time, without any extra effort, right in your living room or bedroom.

There are also three other structural aspects that differentiate the two powerful visual media, cinema and television. First, the idea of timing, scheduling and serialising. The television content is for prolonging suspense. Although its programming is prolonging, its criteria of evaluation with TRPs is instant, or over a week, with no immediate financial consideration.

Second, unlike viewing cinema at earmarked time for the purpose, in the case of viewing a TV set, there are multiple options and choices now.

Third, motivation for television is sponsorship or ability to elicit advertising. The structure of television enterprise is such that it is more directly influenced by the kind of advertising support that can be elicited as that matters and determines the success-failure aspect.

Fourth, in television there is scope for quick correctives and television production are mostly Work in Progress, unlike cinema where once the film is released after certification, no change is possible in the plot or players. And yet, television does not seem to benefit from that flexibility as much because of its TRP-fixation.

Television Research
The Indian Case

ALTHOUGH TELEVISION in India has fifty years' track record, private and competitive television is about twenty-five years old. The way round-the-clock channels have proliferated in India is unprecedented in the world, more than half of them are self-proclaimed 'news channels' No other country has witnessed proliferation of channels so quickly that cut across socio-cultural and economic divides.

It all happened without pertinent government policies and preparations, including without backup of any basic research and training. Also, all such significant development in the country happened without any kind of field research either on viability aspects or on the kind of model of TV content that India should adopt and the kind of implications that television is likely to have, going by the experience of other countries. Even competitiveness between channels was not based on much of research of any type. Also, there was no discourse as to the pros and cons of going for commercialisation of television without any sensitivity to the decentralisation aspects, cross media and monopoly issues and ownership and control aspects. It was in such a free-for-all environment that the TRPs and rating culture penetrated the television scene of India.

Television is a double-edged medium, unlike most other public mass media. *On no other media has so much primary and secondary research been conducted world over as on television. It was realised early enough that effects of television are far greater and has more implications on human behaviours than any others. It was also understood early that creative opportunities are so many.* It was in recognition of its implications that so many field studies were conducted worldwide, in particular in the context of children and women. As early as in 1967, for example, the Annenberg School[1] of Communication (USA) undertook longitudinal study on violence and television. (This writer attended one of the research sessions with Dr George Gerbner in Philadelphia in 1968.) Much earlier, in the early 1960s, it was based on field research that Ford Foundation had sponsored—a classic example of using television for empowering children and in such a way that television lays the foundation much beyond the school system (the *Sesame Street* serial was an outcome). It was a long period of research which suggested cartoon format appeals to children more and which they are likely to retain or recall more, even much after.

Television research had taken roots in USA on two fronts (much before television had engulfed India). Academics of universities (sociology, psychology, anthropology, media, etc.) had taken to fundamental research to do with impact, influence, behavioural change, persuasion, motivation, knowledge and many such aspects.

The Advertising industry prompted research in the power of persuasion, awareness, knowledge and influence research in specific contexts, mostly to do with consumerism, marketing and promotion of brands of various kind. Advertising research took to diffusion of innovations, communication effectiveness and media strategies. Market research firms also took to these research services. However, neither socio-economic nor social development aspects at an aggregate level at the national plane received a special attention in India.

It was Professor Wilbur Schramm[2] at Standford University, one of the early academicians, who took interest in the mid-sixties in developing countries, in the context of media and communication. This pursuit received further boost with Professor Everett Rogers taking to diffusion of innovations research, including in India around 1965. Initially the concern was agriculture and then family planning and health. They were the special context of research pursuit which also gave fillip to research attempts in India. *This research-based entertainment-education idea received wide acknowledgment in mid-1970s* which led to India taking to its first such research-based concept by way of the well-appreciated *Humlog* serial, which ran daily for a couple of years on Doordarshan.

Humlog was the first entertaining family serial on Doordarshan with several social development messages at the initiative of SS Gill, then Secretary Ministry of I&B, who took a delegation to Mexico to adopt the entertainment-education concept in India. By then, *Simple mete Mario* was a classic Mexican serial which had (re) launched the entertainment-education model globally. It was a research-based serial. Manohar Joshi, who authored *Humlog,* was also part of that delegation. More such serials were made thereafter like *Nukkad* and *Udaan.* These were based on pre-post and impact research.

The Satellite Instruction Television Experiment, known as SITE, was a milestone in Indian television with immense potential for India to come up with a model which was appropriate for India. SITE could have been a breakthrough for research-based Indian television, but that model was never followed up. Space Application Centre (of ISRO) in Ahmadabad took several pioneering initiatives to demonstrate how interdisciplinary research could help to develop content strategies for change and development and how impact research could guide television channels proactively. It was based on such research that SITE followed up with the Pij television centre in Gujarat, *but that experiment too was made to end* as it had the potential to offer a viable television model for India.

The first National Readership Survey (NRS) was a turning point (1971-74) in the Indian media scene, when that media research took off in India. But the mind-set and modus operandi of the advertising industry tuned itself to quantification (from subjectivity of earlier years), and computer models and instant formulas for media planning. In that process, awareness creation had become the primary concern rather than change, motivation and futures or any of the national goals and public policies.

The kind of research advertisers looked for until then was of 'supportive' nature, which means limiting to optimisation exercises of efforts, not effects. The research concern was limited to budgets, media planning, media strategies and campaign outcomes. AC Nielsen's readymade model of meter-elicited-instant-data on viewership soon became a business model (for the research corporate) rather than research for change, innovation and entrepreneurship; the assessor gets most out of challenges of contradictions in contents in this process. The focus of advertisers was markets, consumers and brands. That meant a very limited research perspective and constrained methodologies to go about it. *Reach and exposure remained the sole concern of all research on television in India, not impact and change and involvement of people.* Even now, 25 years of competitive television in India has not changed this.

In that process, the TRP idea never took cognisance of India's unique challenges of socio-economic and cultural diversities. A combination of research methodologies would have been a better bet rather than confining to 'ratings'. Even now, it is not too late for BARC to consider and the academics to take on relevant and specific research priorities for a India-specific television model.

Everett Rogers and Arvind Singhal,[3] then of Southern California University, did extensive research through CMS in India for study of the implications for Indian television scene (1994-2004), which included radio and television serials. Impact and implications were their concern for their research.

The positives of television are nowhere evident unless accompanied by pre-, mid-course, post- and evaluative research. Constant monitoring and tracking are a basic primary requirement for television to emerge as a positive and proactive media. Such monitoring is required both from within and outside, independently but with transparency.

But India is an exception. It cannot have such a system even after 25 years of proliferation of channels. In India, copycatting has played a far more active role perhaps because of the quick succession in which phases of growth took place despite brilliance and abundance of creative talent and the many academic institutions in the country. But we have been scratching the surface with ratings. *Instead of concern for fundamentals of research in the context of the unique characteristics of television as a medium, especially in a country like India, we have been on and off raising the issue of 'size of sample', as if this is the only important issue in any national discourse on the media.*

Scope of Viewership

Television research can broadly be in different types and phases. The first, foremost and preliminary is about *reach* of television. That is how many have access (to television and its broadcasts from various sources) and also avail the same and see the contents that are telecast and also available on a particular TV set. Television is installed in one's house for the inhabitants to see as and whenever and whatever, either by choice or otherwise and view actively or passively or casually. While all those in the household can be considered as *potential viewers* of programmes on that television, only those who are actually watching a particular programme at a particular point of time can be considered as *viewers* of that programme or any broadcasts on that television set at that time.

Whether such actual viewing makes any difference on those who view, is altogether different. Any such impact and effects can be ascertained over time, not instantly. The implications or effects by way of making any difference can only be over time.

This effect or impact cannot be reliably measured instantly and by a deduction exercise. Recorded data of television sets by way of *on* and *off* of meters can only be the activity of the set/gadget/television at a particular *point in time*. That is—the number of people who have the potential to view at that point and also watching at the particular time. Considering all such potential individuals as also the viewers of a programme (which could be of some duration) can only be an assumption-based estimation specific to a particular time point. If such assumptions are without research backup, reliability aspect can only be a guess. From a media planner's perspective, the reach variables may be good enough, not so for a channel or programming and larger socio-economic development point of view. For, someone can be considered as viewer only on viewing a programme, not in a passing way or casual way but in an 'active way'.

People who can be reached *over time* and those who have the potential to view at any *specific time* are not the same.

What the meter used initially captured was just whether the television set in the particular selected household was *on* or *not* and for *how long,* assuming the off button was also activated as promptly.

Of course, even for *impact* evaluation of television, one needs to know the *reach*. But that alone is not enough to establish actual viewership. Naturally, viewership by itself is not impact, although that is a first step in that 'process'. These subtle differences cannot be mixed up to suit rating of channels or programmes for a syndicated commercial service as TRP was and imposed as an yardstick for the industry.

The *reach* data that TRP provides weekly has another misinterpretation which has gone unquestioned. This is about the kind of assumptions that are made out of trends in *reach data* from one week to another, or even over the weeks. When a particular hour or programme or a channel is on (even when push button is on for much less than a minute), it is assumed as popular or preferred whereas the reasons can be altogether different in the case of certain sections of households and certain age groups in the household, as in the case of two to eight-year-old children or housewives, for example.

But data on *reach* of television at aggregate level is available from multiple other sources. Periodic National Readership Surveys were the first to provide an idea as to the reach of television in a relative context with other mass media. Then there are periodic surveys in other contexts with even larger sample surveys like the National Family Health Survey, NCAER survey etc.[4] These can be availed more for validating TRP data.

Reach data offered by TAM earlier, and by BARC now, of course, is up to date and with more sensitivity although not in terms of reliability for all contexts and for all section of people of the country. As far as the *reach* aspect is concerned, TRP may not be as reliable as in the case of other sources, as the base of TRP is much limited and restrained but facilitates comparisons within a year and sensitivity to frequent happenings, including context variables.

Since the costs involved in ascertaining *reach* reliably are huge, BARC should reconsider the scope of its 'infrastructure' round of the survey as a part of its Broadcast India Survey.

TRAI had initially debated in its guidelines the difference

between 'market research' and 'rating activity'. Market research implies much beyond the reach aspect and includes the customer or viewer end aspects like consumption, brand preferences etc.

Rating activity does not necessarily include anything beyond quantifying *reach* and *extent of exposure* aspects. TRAI apparently compromised about sufficiency of scope of ratings. TRAI did not envisage perils of rating on creative outcomes and contents and ignored larger aspects involved, including *social impact* implications. TRAI apparently went more by the concerns and interests of advertisers and advertising agencies and also of channels as economic enterprises rather than as mass media having social effects. *Civil society and social institutions of the country were not taken into account during formulating TRAI guidelines for rating methodology.*

A very limited perspective about the very role and relevance of television per se apparently had led to TRAI taking an advertising and advertiser perspective, ignoring larger and long-term implications of viewing television over time and long-term consequences. Even at this late hour, in a proactive initiative, the independent TRAI can take a relook at the guidelines in vogue and take a more comprehensive view of the very concept of viewership and its ratings in a larger context. The rating rankings are based on an inadequate and limited scope methodology and isolated view of a medium with immense potential to influence behaviours and life styles at various levels and even more, over time. TRAI should make *impact research* a periodic obligatory concern of all rating agencies and recommend an appropriate way of providing funds for such impact studies, so that ratings are not viewed in isolation of the larger scene.

Research Objectives

Why viewership estimate is needed in the first instance—for what, to whom and for whose interest? Is it for determining the *reach* or *impact* or as *feedback* to channels and producers? Is it a revenue-generating business or an instrument to influence viewership or both? Can it also be *a developmental support service* to get the best of television media and as a social institution? In what way has ranking based on TRP contributed since the ratings are now of over two decades old? Who has benefited from these TRPs? Why has there been no study of these aspects by anyone? Why is the same methodology of TRP being repeated even after proliferation of these channels and viewership has increased and competitiveness is the overriding factor?

Is the rating about channels or of programme or genres or certain time chunks? Has the same concern and methodology limited viewing opportunity and production and creative opportunities? The scope of methodology has to be beyond meter-centric ratings, if the concern is the larger aspects of TV viewing and its impact. The methodology has to be reliable and representative and should explore to include qualitative aspects (along with reach and extent of viewing).

Channels are using ratings for promoting the channel or/and its time segments or for positioning individual programmes. The fact that Doordarshan never questioned the methodology of ratings is an extreme example of insensitivity. On the other hand, the channels which stood on the top of the ratings pecking order were those who preferred status quo in the methodology. None of the other channels, like Zee, India News, NDTV or India Today was reactive and assertive vis-a-vis ratings.

The advertising agencies are content that ratings 'fit into' their schemes and quantifications and are good enough to come up with justification for their media plans, budgets and allocations.

For example, no one was interested in attitudes, awareness, motivation, knowledge, behavioural aspects and credibility dimensions of television viewing. Some channels and programme producers may be conducting their own internal studies on some of these aspects from time to time. And such reports obviously remain confidential for internal use and are not ever shared. Since such reports are not shared, methodology issues never come under public scrutiny.

Another aspect about which not much is known is what kind of 'briefing' was given to the television households at the time of installing rating meters and whether all members of a household were involved or only one of the members was briefed. And, more importantly, whether *de facto* pushing of the *on* or *off* buttons on the meter was allowed in the case of children by their elders? It would be interesting to also know for what was the gift or incentive given—for allowing the meter to be fitted to the TV or/and for doing on and off regularly every time and by every individual member in the household, or for watching channels at a given time or for certain duration?

TAM has never shared information on the compliance pattern of different members of a television-owning household and also about meters whose data was *not recorded* or/and transmitted to the central control processor every night.

Scope of Research

Any project idea, when taken up for the first time with potential to dictate the future of an industry, agenda of a country and mind-set of its people, the details of the concept and its methodology are expected to be evident to stakeholder pro bono, if not to the larger public since they are also affected by such data directly or indirectly. Even more so in the case of syndicated research projects like rating television viewing. What is viewership all about? When is one considered a viewer? What is proposed to be measured? What are the criteria and cut-offs that determine these notions? Then, of course, are the answers to questions which are not always obvious, like for whom has the measurement been taken up or for whose advantage is it devised? How much about these aspects are in the public domain and updated? If the project has implications for a larger public, then what kinds of mechanisms are there for accountability including for grievance redressal? And is there any conflict of interest involving the promoters and the executing agency?

In the case of TRP, it is important that stake holders know about the key aspects of methodology. These include the size of sample and which phenomena is tracked, how the analysis of captured data is made public, with what frequency such an analysed data is made available to whom and in what kind of format? TRP reports were presented at what intervals and what levels like State, national, metro etc are also relevant information required. But in the case of TRPs, neither the agency concerned nor any of the industry bodies or any government agency had taken the initiative proactively or in response to public criticism, to explain and put in public domain any such information. It was much later (after 2012) that channels started to welcome complaints from viewers, although it was at the instance of the industry body, News Broadcasting Standards Authority.

Who is the respondent or what is the composition of the sample? Is it the head of a family or every member of the family? The three characteristics of sample that matter is size, spread, and selection procedures. The three aspects, of course, are interrelated. How much about these aspects is in public purview? Is there any sub-sample at the selection stage, say of children or of any particular category of respondents? Since viewers size was indicated for age 4 (2 now) plus year's children, the size of this category of sample would be different. There is general impression that more the samples, the merrier, whereas in reality it could be the other way. This obviously depends on what exactly the reports are expected to capture. A 20,000 sample of households could be good enough for insights on TV viewing habits. But to get a more reliable estimate at aggregate national level but in a disaggregated way, one may need beyond 50,000 samples, depending on the spread and selection procedures of the households.

Responses obtained by personal interview with the identified sampled respondents may be more reliable than interview on a phone and that may be more reliable than the one from a meter and even from a people meter and IVR (Interactive Voice Responses).

What is it that is measured in the case of meter-based ratings? Is it the duration that a TV set is on, or the number of times each day or duration each time a channel is looked at or is it in which combination of these aspects is the programme viewed or meter operated?

Was this measurement with 'people meter' for every individual in the sampled television household fitted with the people meter? All this is mechanically recorded but human intervention is there in pushing the TV on and then pushing the assigned button on the meter and, every time, not only push the on but also push the off button every time a person moves away from the TV screen. Neither of these measures, by itself, means actually viewing something on the screen of the television. It is only an indicative factor and one can deduct some conclusion taking into account certain chance factors. The chance factor can be arrived at, based on some qualitative sub (or small) sample studies. It is, however, not known whether any such experiments were carried out by TAM or even by BARC now.

For examples, the number of households where the TV is on but no one is in front actually (although the off button on the meter has not been put off) watching something on screen is a critical operation to factor in. And then, whether the telecast is fully watched or partly or on and off. This criteria depends on, for whose interests or benefit is the exercise carried out? Since the advertiser is key, the cut-off point for considering one as viewer is determined as two minutes each time. Similarly, once it was decided that children are key consumers, below 12 age members in a household were brought under meter regime and then lowered to 7 and then further lowered to 4 years and then to just 2 years. *No one in India is even asking, should two-year-olds be even watching television?* This is despite the fact that the top multinational advertisers never wanted to aim their campaigns at below 12 years age groups.

Another way of describing this phenomenon is, someone may be an active viewer where one sees something on screen at a given point by choice. Someone else may be in the range of the TV screen but passively, s/he may be in conversation with someone or other or engaged in doing something else in which case, watching is more casual but the on button on the meter remains on. Should all such seeing be taken as *viewership* or should the report be separate for each of the three categories of looking at the screen to see a programme? In the case of TAM's TRP it was not clear at the outset which one of the three situations was considered for *viewership.* Is this any different now (2018)?

Then again, for some other fundamental questions for which answers do not come from the meter recording but could come from personal observation or personal interview only. But without clarity and stakeholders knowing about such finalities, TRPs were made the yardstick for the industry without ever indicating the limitations of so deduced (or projected) figures and reliability of each figure (because the sample size varies in each case).

The conclusions one comes up with on viewing preference (of a channel or a programme) will be different, depending on the consistency and periodicity of reporting and analysis. In this, what a daily report reflects will be different than what a weekly report brings out and what an online one indicates. They will be altogether at variance. The reliability of such data cannot be the same. It will be misleading even when one goes with rankings from such meter reporting.

For example, why did channels use a 13-weeks cycle for scheduling serials? Is this to suit the convenience of serial producers or to oblige advertising schedules? Or is it to build up viewership by promotion? That is, the duration of programmes and scheduling is to build up loyalty. Viewership cannot be objective when it is intended to be used to promote or build up viewership. A daily viewership figure can be as misleading as the *Breaking News* from many news channels!

Contents of reports and presentation: The objectives of tracking viewership, or whatever was by that description meant, and who does that analysis influences are factors also at variance. The reporting format and the way the analysis is presented to public cannot be as the agency wishes. It has to follow requirement guidelines.

I faced resistance from advertising agencies (they were one of the sponsors of NRS 1970-72) for placing readers of 'only English publication' at the end of the table, in the case of each language. That meant *exposing huge English bias in Indian advertising*, despite the fact that the English language's reach and English newspapers' reach was only marginal as compared to Indian languages. It was a key revelation of the first NRS and I was at that time able to ensure this position is retained, and eventually it was the NRS finding that changed advertising practices as well as took regional media to newer heights.

Disaggregated viewership and the context were never presented together. Also, effort was, as if to avoid a comparison over time so that 'impact' aspect could not be gone into by anyone else. This was ensured by changing one or other definition or scope of coverage as often and make one year as incomparable with another round in another year and so on.

What is not presented or revealed time to time is often critical and not giving that information is misleading the country. For example, *per cent of non-response* (whatever be the reason) from time to time determines the reliability of what is presented as TRP. And that was why, that information was not given. Such revelations bring out limitation of the TAM methodology.

Rating Without Measurement?

Despite multiplicity of channels and competitiveness, television in India depended from the very outset on the same rating, mostly from a single source (for example, for a year or two in between the merger of INTAM with TAM and winding up of I-map service). The big and small channels, Indian and foreign origin channels, new and older channels and channels of all language and gender depended on the same single syndicated source for basic feedback. And yet so little is known about how primary data was collected by the agency giving the feedback or how it put together data and with what reliability and relevance? So little was known even about the agency (TAM) which was the sole source of the syndicated service. This was almost over a period of fifteen years! No alternative or supplementary methodologies for viewership were experimented with during these years.

The concern in TRP was not so much *impact* or *implications* of contents of channels. It is primarily an estimation of the *reach* aspect by a deduction exercise. The methods used have limited potential for anything more. This is perhaps because the concern is commercial, revenue generation and competition. Television viewing in India, particularly because of the multiplicity of channels of distinct genre, calls for *impact on behaviours* or changes behaviours over time. I argued two decades ago that perhaps channels, as well as the advertisers, do not want *effects* to be brought out for larger public scrutiny. Why has there been no such enthusiasm to analyse *impact*?

The TRP system promoted by TAM does not involve any *measurement* as was claimed. Data and analysis merely on *reach* is not enough for channels to distinguish themselves from each other and make a difference. TRP is promoted as if that is good enough to be in the race! Resourceful channels have to conduct their own inhouse research on programming and behavioural research. Most channels don't spend any or hardly any money on field research for other than subscribing for TAM's TRP service and its analysis. Perhaps this is one reason why channels go for more of the same type of contents and very little for original initiative. This is one of the limitations of TV in India as it has adopted a half-baked semi-western model.

Also, one should be clear of the objective of the channel/ television before syndicated TRPs are availed. Is it a *business proposition* where profit is maximised, and research is used for that purpose or is it a *service* where serving more people and empowering and entertaining them is the criteria? And why are TRPs needed on a weekly basis? Mere looking at the TV screen, which is what meters record, may not be good enough for a weekly analysis. But the *effects* aspect that serials can have should be woven into research design. Even more pertinently. for what different purposes people are tempted to use TV or any channel does not come out of ratings methodology. That is, it is better that television contents interest people as well as, they are also in their interest. *Luring people just for capturing commercials cannot be the sole criteria for rating methodology.*

Television content and viewing, both depend on the objectives of a nation in going for television and the objectives of an individual television channel that research methodology depends. Even the timing and the days in a week of the study covered will determine the methodology. For example, when a mix of channels with different backgrounds are in operation, as usually is the case, rating them using the same sample frame or measurement criteria promotes a rat race instead of promoting healthy competition. The priority, in any case is the viewer interest rather than the advertiser interest.

TAM's mandate for TRP service, as it claimed in its website, was 'advertising and entertainment'. And, it claimed its stakeholders as 'advertisers, ad agencies and media operators'. *Nowhere were viewers mentioned. Neither was content of any television channel or news and current affairs programmes its prime concern.* As such, *a methodology that has no viewer interests as a priority in the monitoring services or meter-centred research cannot be acceptable in a democracy like India.* Yet, this same flawed methodology has again been adopted by another agency, this time a national organisation like BARC.

Is Reach and Exposure the Same?

It is a mystery how meter-recorded data has come to be taken and considered as *viewership*? At the most, it reflects *reach*, not *exposure* to a screen or a programme at a given point of time. Exposure should be an essential condition for viewership. What ORG, the agency which originally (1974-85) talked and experimented on television, did was study viewership, based initially on one-to-one interviews, using recall method and or diary method and a combination of both the methods. At that point of time (pre-1990s), neither INTAM nor TAM had come into being, nor their principles like AC Nielsen or Kantar were in India. It would not have been possible to make people of the country believe that pushing a *on* and *off* button on a panel of a meter linked to television set in a household, would be considered as *viewing* what comes on TV at that given point of time. In reality, many different things/programmes can be viewed at that/one point of time. At the most, an off-on measure can be a surrogate or reflective of viewership. Even an off-on measure is not possible without active cooperation of some households, collaboration of advertising agencies and support of public relations agencies. All that was echoed soon thereafter by television channels themselves. But, since that was the system in vogue in the USA etc. it was adopted as a business model in India.

The misnomer cultivated was such that TRP was supposed to and believed to reflect viewership (per cent of viewers, share of viewers etc). In 2013, when that acronym became passé, TAM tried to promote the acronym TVT (television Viewership in Thousands). But by that time BARC[5] had seized the responsibility and started using the word 'impressions'.[6] Why had no one else even from the academic fields questioned or enquired into how this meter recorded per cent or points could be considered as viewership? Perhaps it was because no one else had heard about or seen the meter or how these TRPs were arrived at or derived.

Marginal Coverage, Maximum Mileage!

Those who criticised TRP some time or other over the years did so mostly regarding the size of sample of households covered with meters. The criticism was not so much on other considerations, which equally matter in judging reliability and relevance of viewership ratings. Even those who were critical of sample size did not question the representative character of metered households being covered. Both size of sample and their TV viewing pattern were not representative of 'normal TV viewing' pattern in the country. Those who later questioned that, for example, 10,000 sample was small for a nation of 2.2 billion people and not good enough, had never talked of the fact that initially, when the idea of TRP was promoted, the sample size was hardly a couple of thousand households and limited to a couple of metro cities. In fact, with 10,000 samples one can at least bring out 'a trend' in looking at a TV screen, if not ranking of channels or programmes. Even at 30,000 samples of TV households with meter, the margin of error is upward of 20 per cent, depending on the segment of households and the time of the day.

Sample size in any field survey is based on the kind of accuracy or reliability expected. If one goes strictly by this theoretical logic, TAM was never concerned about accuracy nor reliability of its TRPs. Perhaps it wanted more to sway the trend or set the agenda for Indian TV with some data backup that helps promote propositions with commercial interests. Despite low accuracy and significantly unreliable data, TAM went ahead and very successfully managed to promote and promoted its TRP system for television in India.

TAM never denied the fact that TRPs were for urban gatherings and limited to cities, and initially not reflective of even urban India. But it allowed, and even encouraged news media, to create a make-believe scenario that its ratings were a statement of the 'national TV scene. It was a few years later, after the idea of TRP faced o criticism that TAM extended its metered panels to smaller cities (after 1996-97). It is not in public knowledge that certain parts of the country like Bihar, Assam and North East, for example, were not at all covered until after 2014, as if these populations did not exist before. But much before, by 2000, TRP had already entrenched itself as the currency of the television industry. The fact that rural India and small cities and towns were not at all covered by TAM, and that its data could never have been the benchmark as TRP's were made out to and relied on, never drew media or government attention. Even going by the number of TV sets in the country, coverage of TAM was limited, its sample never kept up with the expanding universe of Indian households owning television nor with the number of channels and change in the delivery mode(from terrestrial to cable and to DTH, for example).

Channels, however, were prompted to go by TAM ratings as if they were the yardsticks for the kind of contents that *channels should focus on* and *stand out* in the viewership rating. It promoted programming that *they presumed* will sustain viewership and give advantage in the rat race between channels for advertising revenues. This trend led to promotion and telecasting of 'more of the same' phenomena of content.

While most advertising agencies, advertisers and channels appeared happy with TAM and its ratings (thanks to its public relations) by about 2005 public criticism of programmes of channels started sporadically, coming from some concerned citizens and civic society groups. It took another few years for criticism to gain sufficient ground to criticise certain contents, particularly portrayal of women, families and the kind of divisive relationships shown in TV serials and for showcasing such serials as 'popular'.

It was this building up of pressure on channels that led to TAM increasing its coverage marginally. It was after the CMS meet at India International Centre in 2007, where both TAM and I-map were made to open up their systems and share the methodology in the presence of past and the then secretaries of I and B Ministry, TRAI representatives and some opinion makers, that Minister Jaipal Reddy appeared interested in how ratings came. Thereafter, it was more because of questions in the Parliament mostly from the Left Parties and their women's wings that TAM figures began to be questioned.

The sample of households covered with meters for rating was motivated. They were prepared and induced to watch channels and use the push off and on buttons of a specially installed meter in lieu of a honorarium or gifts the ratings agency offered. The TAM sample was strictly not even representative of TV households. There was no *choice* criteria, although the agency claimed pre-selection of household for installing the meter based on socio-economic parameters. Initially, the TAM survey was limited to just two metros (Mumbai and New Delhi) with around 500 households, the results of such monitoring was reported in news media as if they were representative of TV viewers in the cities and reflective of the country.

Two key questions are still relevant. First how many meters in TV households, in fact, were in operation or effectively function (during 1994-98) at any given time point and week at that time. With what promptness or accuracy in a day did every member in the household push the off and on buttons assigned? Then, of course, how many meters were non-functional for some other technical reason at any given time point? This 'no signal' could be above ten per cent of metered TV households. And then another question is, which particular socio-economic households were those non-functional households, each time. Obviously, this 'no signal' households at any given point of time have telling implications on the projections made of the findings, from out of the other metered TV households with their percentage varying week to week.

Presentation and Periodicity

Periodicity of TRP releases and the process of compiling TRPs determine the implications of rating services. How primary data is captured, put together or integrated, analysed in a dis-aggregated way, and the frequency of making it available determines how the scores and ranking are being utilised. How that rankings is presented before the public or advertised and how the same is availed by different channels and advertising agencies makes a difference. How much of viewership analysis is syndicated and client specific is also significant. TAM was using the ratings for offering special services to channels which subscribed specially. TRP has implications much beyond the interests of subscribers. It has a fallout that affects viewers (policy agencies and academics). Competitive compulsions are yet another consideration that gets covered in public media, spontaneously and promoted specially. The more the competition between subscribers, the more sensitive the process of compiling TRPs becomes. What kind of 'third party' validation, the TAM process was put to is another aspect that matters for the credibility of the ratings. But the TAM process and formula of TRP had never gone through an independent validation. As a private limited company TAM has always been on a profit maximisation course. BARC, being a non-profit agency, need not fall into such traps.

Rating and ranking or even positioning of a channel or programme or time segment acquires credibility, based on the kind of transparency with which various processes involved go through. The way the exercise is planned, executed, presented and *objectivity* of the tools used for each of those stages should matter and also be evident.

Data recorded on push off and on buttons on the meter in the metered TV households is captured by a central server every night and collated for the day or week days and analysed in a disaggregated way and presented on an agreed format of the report. Whether there was any such an understanding with subscribers beforehand in the case of TAM service is not known.

Since manipulation of data at any of these stages cannot be ruled out, it is critical that checks and third party validation is built into the system. When an American President talks of 'fake news' and a President-elect talks about manipulation that change the course of the nation, why no leader in India ever talked about the way TRPs were presented as reliable in the news media and hyped by channels themselves for over so many years?

Realising that channels were misusing TRP reports, BARC at the very outset of release of its own reports, issued an advisory to subscribers on how they should take the ratings and how they could claim results that were not true or exaggerated. Despite advice, however, channels have not moderated their often-exaggerated and misleading claims week after week. The fact that even after BARC's advise in the interest of channels themselves, some channels went berserk with claims of 'No 1' position in BARC's rating week after week tells us much about the channel's mindset. It is amusing to see how English news channels in particular claim week after week that each one is 'No 1 always', 'Undisputed channel No 1', 'No 1 with real numbers', 'Prime Time No 1', 'With maximum Prime time audience' etc. Some give the percentage (what that percentage is representatives of is not indicated clearly) of competitive channels. Channels also indulge in claiming how their coverage of certain events (may be assembly election or cricket etc.) is 'most viewed' or 'highest viewed'. All of them site BARC source, just like, once upon a time they quoted TAM. Some refer to certain 'markets' or certain 'age groups', or gender as a part of the source. Earlier this was disputed as Wednesday Favour, now it is called Friday favour. It was a mystery how competing channels claimed in advertisements in their respective channels, number one position, quoting the same source and same position in the rankings and rating.

Together, some channels, advertisers, TAM (earlier) and public relations corporates, promoted TRPs as the ultimate solution for viability. Public relations agencies played a key role in keeping up this performance. *When Prasar Bharati suggested to TAM/AC Nielsen that they should specifically mention that their ratings were limited to certain section or regions, and that figures were subject to margin of error, TAM did not comply.* Prasar Bharti had already released a few crores of rupees of pending subscription to TAM and nothing could force TAM to oblige.[7]

Allegations of fudging data and manipulation of analysis or TRP releases have been surfacing in the last decade. Initially it was not known what the TRPs were all about and how they were arrived at and what was the sample. The first charges were, therefore, that members of households were being advised informally by the agency and offered gifts etc. to watch certain channels or and certain programs or for certain duration.

Awards, Yet Another Add-on!

TAM never even experimented during its two decades of TRP service with any alternative or supplementary method to meter recording of television's reach and exposure – nothing of that kind was ever made known to the public. Even to validate meter ratings, TAM did not try *recall* in any personal interview method, or in a diary method or by way of a telephonic interview or by taking recourse to IVR technology. There was no indication that TAM had ever undertaken any study even with a small sub-sample.

Realising certain vacuum and irrelevance of TRPs, I first wrote in a daily newspaper and some periodical publications about inadequacy of the meter recorded ratings. Finding no takers on any of the basic issues involved in the very idea of meter recorded viewership and the very methodology for the weekly ratings, I initiated an award to television channels and programmes on the basis of certain good practice. Not as an alternative to TAM's TRPs but as an independent validating and supplementary forum. After consulting with independent professionals like Shyam Benegal who at that time was the Jury Chief of *CMS Vatavaran* film festival[8] (which now continues for the sixteenth year where films on any of the elements of nature are awarded by an independent Jury), the CMS television award was instituted in 2006.

As a proactive initiative, CMS awards to 24-hour news channels in Telugu (which continue to be large in numbers of channels – 20 in the country next only to Hindi), neither accepted any sponsorship nor took any fees for including a channel for consideration of awards. There was no practice of taking entries from channels for a consideration. Of course, channels were welcomed to submit their programmes which they considered deserve public recognition. The Telugu news channels were first independently monitored and viewed by a panel of experts and analysed and then considered for awards by yet another final jury of eminent and active personalities on the basis of certain criteria identified, based on CMS field studies over the years and insights of Jury members. These criteria were shared with channels in an open workshop six months before the Jury met. At the time of the awarding ceremony, why the awards were being given to a particular channel or why a programme was considered for the award was explained by the Jury Chief. These awards and the criteria have nothing to do with TRP ratings. In fact, the Jury did not take into account these ratings. Even the gala awards ceremony was not offered for sponsorship.

After three years of CMS awards to Telugu news channels, a National Television Awards was started by a Bombay-based website journalist in 2011-12. Another magazine too started awards to TV channels two years later and while both these awards continued as commercial activities, CMS stopped its awards to news channels, on finding the response of news channels lukewarm. CMS discontinued its awards in 2012, after realising that channels prefer awards where there is scope for manoeuvres, rather than something which is independent, transparent and cannot be meddled with. Realising the potential of awards, UNICEF came along in support of the CMS award for the next five years (2012-17). It wanted to give the awards to general entertainment channels to motivate them to take to social development issues.

Both, the News Television Awards (NTV) and Exchange4media Awards (ENBA), are now a decade old. What has been their impact? Have they made any difference? The two awards have become money spinners for the promoter and trumping opportunities for channels. For, both awards are sponsor- driven and for every entry, a channel has to pay a fee. Whichever channel pays more, its chances for an award are more. The one which does not file its nomination accompanied by the fees, does not even figure for the awards consideration.

No criteria are known, nor is there any transparency in the selection process. Although the jury is changed every time, it is not independent and with the conflict of interest is obvious. That was how, crime based serials, which are considered distasteful in personal discussions with viewers are the ones awarded. In the process, these awards echo the TRP culture. As public relations exercise, these awards have been perpetuating the content model that the TRP system had popularised in the previous decade. For channels, these awards remain self-aggrandising opportunities.

No wonder, Narayan Rao, then vice-president of NDTV said as chief guest at the NTV Awards function in 2012 that the 'channels need to come out of deceptive policies in the name of reaping the best of their potential'. He further observed that such awards should not become 'yet another mistake' in consolidating the strength of channels.[9] It was like Sachin Tendulkar's advice while honouring Saina Nehwal on her winning a Bronze medal at the Olympics in 2012, 'the world is yet to see the best'. And he suggested that the 'best is yet to come' view is far more durable and takes one to newer heights. Such a view is even more true in the case of television channels engaged in cut-throat competition and self-aggrandisement with claims of 'the best', 'No.1', 'most viewed' etc. TRP and awards should not drive channels to such deception.

The Key Suspects

AN INDUSTRY service available syndicatedly, as in the case of television viewership measurement, is expected to be independent, transparent and a credible support particularly because channels are of varied category, highly competitive, spread across languages and constantly going through changes in their scope, structure, technology and size. The TRP service in India came into vogue, piloted by an agency riddled in conflict of interest and operating as a profit-driven private limited company, with its ownership and control remaining abroad. The front of this agency, TAM, remained with the same person, LV Krishnan, staying as its CEO all through the years,1985-2017.

TAM

Apart from TAM and BARC, more recently a few other agencies too are involved directly or indirectly, supporting or moulding the structure of the viewership rating service in India. These include TRAI, Star TV, ORG, MARG, Doordarshan, and CMS. And yet TAM remained as a monopoly enterprise (until BARC took responsibility). It is still not clear who was accountable and responsible for any questions or grievances on any specific aspect of TRPs by any stakeholder? Did anyone know the credentials of TAM to address any queries? TAM had never gone through the kind of public scrutiny in its earlier years as BARC has been, since it launched its operations.

TAM Media Research India Pvt Ltd (TAM) should be complimented for what it accomplished in a matter of less than a decade. What the Indian government could not do to make a difference in two decades in changing the scope and course of television in India, TAM did that in a decade. It not only changed the direction but mesmerised television channels, unleashed a wave of upworldly mobile content and made viewers addict to a new genre of serials scoring over otherwise strongly entrenched feature films and film-based models until then.

The public face of TAM continued to be that of one individual, and his one-to-one public relations skills were such that he was synonymous with TRPs. As CEO of TAM (1985-2018), he managed its affairs single-handily. But now it is the service provider BARC, and not so much Partho Dasgupta, its CEO, that the rating service is known as. One does not still know how much the public or even the stakeholders know even in 2018 about the origin of viewership ratings as a service in the public domain, the process of growth and background of agencies associated or involved in viewership ratings of television channels and programmes. It is pertinent even now to have an idea about that shadowy past and about those various agencies involved.

If TAM had done what its successor (BARC) did in November 2016[1] by suspending (although temporarily) three channels from its system of meter-based tracking of viewing, TRP would not have gone out of its control.

BARC found practice of tampering meters and confirmed that from an 'unusual behaviour pattern' in viewership trends as a result of 'all of a sudden watching' of certain channels during certain hours. This was exactly what had happened in the initial years when AC Nielsen ORG MARG took to meter-based monitoring of viewership and popularised a new content model for television in India, when (1992-95) only a few knew of metered TV households and what it all meant to television in India. As Nielsen found takers for its quantified monitoring as *viewership* ratings, they registered TAM as an Indian company in 1998 taking along IMRB/Kantar as an associate.

By taking over ORG and MARG, Nielsen acquired a wide range of data bases and field research capabilities. They could find subscribers quickly and the support of those who matter for market domination. That is, multinational marketing and advertising companies, who had entered the Indian market in a big way, irrespective of whether they were previous clients of Nielsen elsewhere or not, supported TRPs as that was how television viewership was being tracked in USA. Similarly, Indian advertising agencies who by then became foreign controlled and those foreign agencies who had come to India with their local associate in public relations, market research and media planning services, also supported TAM's TRP. Using ORG's data bases of two decades, client base and Indian standing, Nielsen quickly managed to take control of the Indian scene. L Krishan who headed TAM from the outset has been a fantastic public relations expert. He helped consolidate TAM's dominance of the television landscape in all its dimensions. He promoted TRPs as if they are synonymous for popularity, a solution for viability of channels and made channels themselves believe that.

IMRB, the other market research outfit already a key player in India, had also come up with a TV viewership monitoring service. Nielsen quickly came to terms with the principles of IMRB, Kantar, which meant merger of TAM and INTAM in India, but the impression given was that they merged 'at the instance of the industry'. The other compulsion for merger was inconsistencies in the rating and ranking between the two different TRP services and increase in doubts regarding the ratings and their reliability.

TAM's positioning strategy paved a highway for it! It presented itself as 'by invitation', and then 'on request' of advertising and television industry of the country and as if TAM's operation was in 'consultation' with the industry. Once that was claimed, it started describing itself as 'neutral' and 'independent', although it was a private limited company and its corporate links (of Nielsen and Kantar) were so obvious and even when it was well known that TAM is a company for profit maximisation. TAM's (or its principal's) links with advertising agencies and market research and public relations firms as businesses collaborators was known (in the circles) and helped TAM's penetration and helped consolidate its position in India.

Initially, the corporate identity of Nielsen in India was ORG and MARG, which had developed their own credibility over 20 past years. And then it became AC Nielsen-ORG-MARG. And then finally it was known as AC Nielsen on its own. At one point, for a year or two perhaps until legal formalities in India were complete, they were soliciting research assignments in separate names even when they were operating as one legal entity. That was how the legacy of the Indian market research pioneers (ORG and MARG) were usurped. Kantar, on the other hand, continues to describe itself as a partner of TAM India and as Kantar/IMRB.

Who owns AC Nielsen and Kantar internationally? Their shareholding in TAM India is known as 51:49. But globally who owns them was not clear a decade ago, nor until 2015. That helped TAM to escape charges of conflict of interest.

Not everyone who heard of TAM, knew what it actually stands for? However, they all know about TRP, its product that TAM made a household name. Is it Television Advertisement Measurement (as it was originally)? Or is it Television Audience Measurement? Does TRP consider all *viewers* as *audience*? And, all those who push a button of the meter in the radius of a TV set in the household are *viewers,* even if that was for one minutes or less! A TRP culture was infused not only into the Indian media scene but into Indian public discourse as a reliable concept. By whom? When? How? Several such questions arise. On 7 March 2007, TAM's Krishnan let go an opportunity to be transparent on several such apprehensions at the CMS round table on 'Television Viewership Measurement Dilemma and Challenges'.[2] He did not even bring the meter being used despite request to demonstrate its operations. (See Annexture).

According to the TAM website, TAM sponsors included Grey advertising, J Walter Thomson Advertising and Young and Rubicon, also advertising. The three world's leading ad agencies together were the big three of advertising industry in the early nineties in the USA and UK. Their main agenda, as per their website, was market research, media, entertainment industry, advertising, public relations and consumer insights. They claimed to have advertisers, media owners, advertising agencies as their clientele. Nowhere did they refer to or indicate viewers as a stakeholder.

Although it was registered as TAM India Private Limited only in 1998 as an Indian company for profit, TAM actually began operations in this country in 1991-92 as an informal outfit of AC Nielsen-ORG-MARG. While Nielsen was a global leader on its own as a market research corporate outside India (it was reluctant to enter India on my personal invite as president of ORG in 1982), it soon discovered India's numbers and came to India in the nineties on its own. The thirty-year-old ORG, as the foremost market research outfit in India, had a range of databases as it was already by then offering a wide range of services to the Indian media, markets and advertising community. IMRB had come to India in 1970 as an outfit of the British Market Research Bureau (BMRB). To consolidate TAM India, its Indian company with its TRP service, Nielsen aligned with another premier European market research company, Kantar Media whose Indian associate IMRB was another leading market research outfit in India. While ORG and MARG, the Indian agencies, were taken over by AC Nielsen and their identities wiped out, IMRB continues to be active as a market research and advisory services.

It is important to know TAM's origins to understand the motivations of TRP and its objectives. Of course, to get to know the origins, we need to go beyond AC Nielsen, Kantar, Grey, J Walter and Rubicon advertising and to Martin Sorrell. TAM was supposed to have merged with INTAM in 2001 at the instance of customers so that they do not have to subscribe to two different rating services. But the compulsions were otherwise. The first was the merger or coming together of AC Nielsen and Kantar abroad. Of course, AC Nielsen was taken over later by another conglomeration VNU. The other compulsion was the worry that INTAM and TAM were often clashing in their interests, with same target clients and with two different set of projection figures, creating doubts in the reliability of both the services. INTAM was floated as a rating service in the previous couple of years by ORG-MARG, on their coming together a year earlier at the instance of *Business India*'s Ashok Advani. Advani soon sold control of his companies to AC Nielsen. Indians were mere pawns in this larger corporate world games.

Little was known about Kantar Media Research until 2013-14, although it was half owner of the TV ratings (TAM) in the previous two decades. Its Chairman, Eric Salama, visited India and hit headlines in December 2013 when he announced that Kantar was interested in continuing with TAM's rating service together with Nielsen as its partner. Then, once the government became aware, the government stepped in and issued an Executive Notification, stipulating conditions for compliance. Kantar then filed a case in the Delhi High Court against the Union Government's notification on rating agencies, which disqualified TAM as a rating agency.

It is because of the hold that Kantar and its principals (the WPP Group of Martin Sorrell) continue to have on advertising and the advertising agency business that TAM's TRPs took such deep roots in India. Kantar group's known associates in India include Group M, O & M, JWT, IMRB, Bates and TAM. Partnering with Nielsen (India) Pvt Ltd and its associates—all engaged in media and advertising enterprises—together they dominate the practices and priorities, including in the case of contents of television channels, curtsey TRPs. That was why Kantar challenged the government's regulation on rating and cross-media holding provisions that the executive notification brought in. The guidelines in the notification endangered Nielsen-Kantar priorities. Delhi High Court, however, did not agree to stay the government's notification.

Conflict of interest was obvious and blatant in TAM's pursuit of ratings. Until TRAI came up with guidelines for television rating in 2013, TAM was operating through its own units or subsidiaries like TAM Media Research Pvt Ltd, Ad Ex India (renamed ORG service which ORG had initiated and ran for 20 years earlier) and Ei Ko PR Monitor, and its sponsor AC Nielsen was operating throughout this time separately, using TAM data. All this happened until TAM formed a separate company, the Meter Management Company, to plug into BARC which had launched its operations in 2013, although it was legally registered in 2010 (as suggested by the Amit Mitra Committee and TRAI).

I had written about INTAM/TAM's initial experiments in 1991-92 with 250 meters in Mumbai and then 400 in Delhi and Mumbai. By 2003, the number of meters deployed in the country was less than 5,000. TAM took more than another decade to double that number of meters as public pressure was building up against its meagre sample size. Even in 2013, it had only 12,000 metered households as its sample size.

Neutrality and Broadcast Audience Research Council

Although BARC was registered in 2010, how come it took almost five years to come out with any report and that too, only after it reached an understanding in 2013-14 with TAM? *What role did TAM and its principals play to ensure delay in the taking-off of BARC?* Five years is a long time in the life of TRPs. Even after that, BARC was not sure of its service schedule until it had an agreement with TAM's Meter Management Unit in February 2016. It has agreed that the TAM meters will continue in the field and will continue to operate with its all other services to media and advertising enterprises, including rating radio contents and other media and monitoring or the advertising flows. And it is TAM who is supplying to BARC, the programme schedules of channels telecasting in India, so that BARC can match its ratings.

It is time, BARC starts to assert its difference and India-concern. It is eight years old.

TAM operations cannot be said to be as transparent as expected of such operations. For example, the meter was neither publicly demonstrated (as CMS did with its meter in Bangalore and Delhi in 1991) nor was its methodology with minimum details in the public domain ever. BARC has at least put its methodology on its website. *It is still a mystery as to what exactly is BARC's understanding with TAM and why a joint company (called Meter Management) had to be formed?* Has TAM withdrawn its case in the Delhi High Court against BARC?

The Economic Times tells the story of BARC

BARC was being propelled as an alternate TV viewership measurement system to the incumbent, TAM Media Research. TAM, a 50:50 joint venture between Nielsen and Kantar Media, was responsible for the ratings that decide the fate of the Rs 22,000 crore spending on TV advertising.

TAM was unable to capture 'What India Watches'. The number of TAM 'people meters', the boxes that collect the viewership data, were inadequate to cover the vast footprint of India.

Government asked TRAI – India does not have a broadcast regulator – to come up with the guidelines for TV ratings agencies. On 11 September 2013, TRAI made public the guidelines after a lengthy consultation process. BARC began exploring the possibility of taking Kantar on board. The aim was to get both Nielsen and Kantar, research consultancies, on board as vendors for research, planning, designing etc.

Nielsen was willing to be a part of the new system but as part of the JV agreement with Kantar, it could not have entered the Indian market on its own. 'You Indians can never do it', the global head of Kantar Media bluntly told the media professional, referring to BARC's ability to create a TV ratings system.

Unbeknownst to him at that time, the Kantar top boss' outburst would set in motion a chain of events that would change the Indian TV ratings system forever. BARC would eventually create the world's largest viewership measurement system, involving 22,000 panel homes and employing a disaggregated model with over 30 vendors in less than two years.

Partho Dasgupta, CEO of BARC, visited London where he met representatives of a French company called Mediametrie. By then, Dasgupta, BARC chairman Punit Goenka, who is CEO Zee Entertainment, and Shashi Sinha, CEO, IPG Mediabrands, had decided that they would create a new system come what may.

in April 2015 BARC finally launched the first set of data. Later, individual ratings were launched and things started moving rapidly. Around the same time, clients began to terminate their contracts with TAM. The agency put on a brave face, publishing data despite few takers. But funding ha.

Sir Martin Sorrell, CEO, WPP, the media agency that owns Kantar, saw that options for TAM had run out. India was too big a market to ignore. He met top bosses at Nielsen in June 2015. 'Once Sorrell sprung into action, discussions happened at a lightning speed', observers said. Finally, it was decided that Kantar and Nielsen would join as junior partners of a company that will supply raw data to BARC.

TAM was accused of practicing as a monopoly service. TAM claimed that its TRPs were a solution for viability of channels, thereby luring them take to the TRP service. It also suggested to some clients to engage the services of its subsidiaries to advise the channels how they could use the TRP service and even how a channel could build its rank in TRP. These accompanying services TAM continues to sell, even after BARC took over the ratings business.

The TAM-BARC case went to the CCI (The Competition Commission of India, formerly the Monopoly Commission of India). *TAM has always claimed that it was invited to take up ratings services by the industry, a claim that has never been substantiated or supported.* In fact, neither of TAM's claims that it was independent, or invited by the industry or it being a neutral service were substantiated or endorsed by the industry leaders. Not even its claim that TRP includes 'behaviour' aspects of viewing has ever been validated or supported. How come, the IBF (Indian Broadcast Foundation), the Advertising Agencies Association (AAA) and the Indian Society of Advertisers (ISA) which have backed BARC and even committed to fund BARC, never made such an endorsement of TAM? What TAM was quantifying was *when* people in TV households looked at the TV screen by pushing the off or on button on the meter panel. How could the industry have invited a company (TAM) which had no *locus standi* (earlier it was ORG and MARG and, of course, IMRB) in the industry in India? Who will believe TAM was invited by the industry? ORG, for example, had a joint committee with representation from the Advertising Agencies (AAA), the Advertisers (ISA) and the media organisation Audit Bureau of Circulation (ABC) when it launched the first National Readership Survey (1970-72).

Story of Doordarshan, India's Public Broadcaster

The story of Doordarshan (DD) needs to be specially treated in the context of TAM's TRP and how Indian TV was side-lined in favour of a foreign content model. As of 1995, when TAM was in its initial stage of penetration into India, Doordarshan had completed two decades as India's public service broadcaster, but under the direct control of the government. Although started with two channels as a terrestrial broadcaster, Doordarshan[3] had 100 Kendras or stations (in 2017) operating across the country in major regional languages of the country and had viewers in every nook and corner with penetration among all sections of the country.

Doordarshan adapted to new delivery/distribution options rather quickly as it did with DTH. Until then, it was the only television service available, particularly to rural India, both in terms of reach and also viewership. Its mission being education, information and entertainment, including programmes specially aimed at children, Doordarshan had a bit of everything in its content package. Doordarshan enjoyed special treatment as all registered cable networks were required to include any two of Doordarshan channels in their package besides Lok Sabha and Rajya Sabha channels.

A simple quantitative estimate indicates that viewership to Doordarshan channels and to some of their programmes was much higher than any other channel that was shown in the 1990s, and *it had to be at the top* of the TRP rate lists. Strangely, Doordarshan never questioned the TRPs formally or even casually. Nor did any academic body raise the red flag on the subject of ratings until 2002.

As it came under the open-competition scenario, Doordarshan began to slip from its dominant viewership position despite its loyal viewers as the contents of its channels became monotonous and dull when the medium became very dynamic. With availability of private channels with more strategically devised schedules and promoted programmes, Doordarshan lost viewers. That trend was exploited further by TAM's public relation experts with tracking of television viewing with an on and off meter fixed in a few households. Households having TV for a longer time are likely to look at the new channels and new productions more enthusiastically and this trend was what TAM cashed in on, showing Doordarshan with lower and declining viewership. As a public service broadcaster, Doordarshan obviously suffered because it came with certain mandate and restrains stipulated by the government and had no resilience mechanism in place.

Under such circumstances, TAM exploited the situation to plug into a vacuum almost instantly. Its TRP system was from the very beginning geared to demolishing the national broadcaster, Doordarshan, slowly but steadily and visibly, also causing more pressures from within as it witnessed decline in advertising revenue. For allowing such a situation to happen uncontested, Doordarshan itself should be more blamed. *In fact, Doordarshan's promoter, the government of India, should be held completely responsible for its lack of understanding of the dynamics of the medium and grasp of the competitive media scene. Instead of supporting the national telecaster, the then government even cut its budget allocations and gave deadlines to catch up. At the same time, the successive governments allowed private channels with absolutely no restraints while, at the same time, the kind of constraints that Doordarshan had to face were publicly discussed.* All this facilitated TAM's TRPs to emerge as key driver for the priorities and strategies of foreign-backed television channels where their profits went abroad. *Doordarshan cannot be absolved of its passive stand when it was the victim of a larger scheme to capture Indian markets.* Private channels and the rating agency knew that unless the national broadcaster is belittled and cornered, entrenchment of a model of broadcasting with an altogether different structure and priorities was not possible with the limited networks they had. In this process no one questioned TAM's TRP scheme and its relevance in the Indian context. Advertisers with reasons for increasing their budgets and diverting outlays for television were happy that they no longer had to rely on only DD, and private and foreign channels hoped that their wish to contain DD's monopoly becomes successful.

Doordarshan had peaked its viewership with feature films and film song-based programmes, then with epics like *Ramayana* and *Mahabharata* and then even with serials like *Humlog* and *Udaan*. But as serials of new private channels were more glamorous and their themes were based on deviant behaviours which tend to attract attention, viewership moved out of DD to private channels. More importantly, they promoted products aggressively, luring viewers with gifts and the like with the help of PR experts. Glamour and glitter, twists and turns, unending serialisation and new production and promotional techniques were relied on as if that was the character of television. New techniques of building suspense for viewing the 'next episode' and the next were additional attractions. Whereas Doordarshan, caught in bureaucratic tangles, was neither quick nor engaged in experimentation. During these years, the Secretary of the Ministry and the CEO of Prasar Bharati and the Director General of Doordarshan were often on different courses and wave lengths.

DD vs Star and Sony!

It will be interesting to recall the rating for the first round of INTAM's TRP. Public service broadcaster Doordarshan's programmes, particularly the serials of the time like *Humlog, Buniyad, Nukkad, Udaan, Rajini*, had more viewing-families than any of the serials of any other channel simply because reach and availability of Doordarshan was much higher and widespread, not only in rural areas but across India. When private channels proliferated with luring contents, Doordarshan slipped in its viewership base in the households where private channel options were reliably available.

But this, of course, did not mean that the serials of new channels, however attractive they were, had from the very start higher viewership (in 1990-94) than DD during those early years. But that was what TRPs showed, somewhat like political parties claim or promise on the eve of an election. A very popular weekly programme, *Rajini,* which created ripples in the market on consumer rights and citizen activism was dropped as the sponsoring ad agency backed out (the agency went out of Indian control soon). Why did they back out? If a programme of public service loses sponsorship, should the channel drop it despite the fact that serial had impressive viewership and talked-about impact (consumer activism in the markets as reported in news media)? What did this Doordarshan behaviour show? Was it a channel belonging to a banana republic? Doordarshan news in later years engaged a public relations agency to promote some of its programmes.

The betrayal of Priya Tendulkar, the producer and actor of *Rajini*, is well known. There may be other such instances, not known to the public, that might have occurred. However, thereafter, programmes against consumerism were discouraged in many ways by all TV channels. Not reflecting any such serial's popularity on the TRP list was one such powerful way of sending out the message that *anti-consumerism was to be discouraged and consumerism was to be applauded.* Revenues would come only from product promotion. One can imagine the kind of influence such examples had on channel operators whose dependence on advertiser was all out. No wonder there has been no example of any such provocative programme like *Rajini* on any of the channels since TRP became the measure of viewership in India.

When I took up the seriousness of the matter with the Director General of Doordarshan (Mr Rthikanth Basu), he just did not bother and, on the contrary, he wanted to go along with the advertising industry and continued with unquestioned support to TAM service despite what it meant to DD. It was a glaringly irresponsible act of a senior officer of the government, and his seniors in the I&B Ministry too took a passive stand. My taking up the issue further with the Secretary and the Minister did not make a difference either. I could not wake them up. The Director General of DD soon after resigned from the government to take up the job of CEO of Murdoch's channel in India, Star TV. He took away with him a couple of other senior DD executives too! To quote a 1997 report *From The Magazine:*

> At a glitzy party in New Delhi to launch Star TV's latest serial Gaatha, one question rose above the polite chit-chat.
>
> Was Rathikant Basu, Star's high-profile CEO, looking for a new job? He turned up an hour late - after many had assumed he had chickened out - put up a brave front but declined to throw light on his latest problem: a government missive dated August 11 asking him to resign within 72 hours.

A former Doordarshan (DD) director-general, Basu said he had received a letter signed by Deputy Secretary N Sivasailam of the Department of Personnel and Training only on August 18. In it he was charged with the following:

- Violating the All India Service rules that prohibit civil servants from accepting jobs within two years of retirement unless they have government permission.
- 'Illegally' negotiating for his job at Star while still in government service. The CBI, it is rumoured, is investigating whether Basu's resignation from DD on September 30, 1996 and his signing up with Star the next day were against the rules.
- Disclosing 'government secrets of strategic and sensitive nature', since he had been secretary in the Department of Electronics when he retired.

After a couple of years, in 2006, another CEO of Prasar Bharati invited me to discuss the issue of unfair representation of Doordarshan by TAM with its senior executive from Singapore along with the Indian Chief. This CEO later, significantly, just before his retirement, quietly released a few crore of rupees to TAM without waiting for TAM to do the promised course correction vis-à-vis DD. Doordarshan continued as a subscriber of TAM rating service. That was how the saga of Doordarshan and its setbacks in the market continued for years.

Paradoxically, Bhaskar Gosh, after retirement, described TAM's TRP in a CMS meet in 2007 as a 'great menace' for 'good TV' in the country.

Doordarshan, like All India Radio, had the support of in-house audience research, although that was more to analyse spontaneous feedback (from listeners and viewers) being received and conduct occasional localised field surveys. Its Audience Research Director, Chandrashekhar, a sincere professional had come up at one time with a parallel weekly viewer survey and even presented the result on Doordarshan regularly. Those panel surveys (DART) were based on personal interviews and presented weekly on Doordarshan, but not in a comparative context with other channels. And there was no public relations effort to promote DART results. Doordarshan was shy of promoting itself even in a competitive context when other channels were hyping themselves rather aggressively. Doordarshan never engaged a marketing expert (until 2016) despite the fact that an expert committee (of Sunil Sen formerly of Hindustan Liver) suggested engaging strategic marketing services and streamlining its content schedules.

A BBDO advertising agency estimate in 2003 indicated that Doordarshan had 31 per cent of total viewership of all TV channels in the country. That was more than fifteen years ago. No matter, DD could never counter TAM's week after week downgrading of viewership ratings of DD's programmes.[4]

The channels which indirectly belittled Doordarshan serials by ensuring their own larger viewership, tried to acquire the rights for some of DD's serials. Star TV channel, in fact, did succeed in the case of a couple of programmes. Instead of advantage Doordarshan, this is how its disadvantages were showcased using public relations.

Star TV

The story of Star TV and its 25 years in India is not a mystery. It was a strategy, an aggressive and coordinated marketing and positioning strategy. The Indian sky was open for Star, doors of Indian households were wide open and so also the Indian markets without much of an effort.

The messiah, however, was Subhash Chandra the man who changed the face, scope and structure of broadcasting in India.

It was Zee TV's Subhash Chandra who crusaded to bring Star TV's promoters to India on his shoulder. It was Star's satellite transponder that had the capability to reach every nook and corner of India simultaneously which fascinated this Haryanvi entrepreneur. This media czar is now (2018) also a Member of the Indian Parliament.

Thirty years ago, Star was a Hong Kong based company. In 1991, STAR TV was a joint venture between Hutchison Whampoa and Li Ka-shing. Li Ka-Shing's son, Richard, was CEO. In 1992, Rupert Murdoch bought a 64 per cent stake in Star TV for $525 million. Star was originally broadcasting content from Rupert Murdoch's Fox Broadcasting and thus a synergy was envisioned. In 1992 News Corporation purchased 63.6% of STAR for over $500 million, followed by the purchase of the remaining 36.4% on 1 January 1993. In early '90s, Star India included Star Plus (then an English-language entertainment channel), Prime Sports (later became Star Sports), MTV (through a tie up with Viacom), Star Movies and Zee TV (belonging to Subhash Chandra). Today, Star India Private Limited is one of India's largest media conglomerates, based in Mumbai. The network reaches approximately 720 million viewers a month across India and more than 100 countries. Star India generates more than 30,000 hours of content every year and broadcasts 120+ channels.

Once Star was taken over by Murdoch, it was TRP which

became the Garuda (the bird of Lord Vishnu) of Star TV in India and positioned the group, propelled its popularity and ensured it was on the top of the rating pyramid, led as it was by the able Peter Mukherjea, now (2018) in jail. He was not only politically and financially influential, he pulled a heavy media punch.

It would not be wrong, therefore, to speculate, was it just a coincidence that the rise of Star TV and the idea of a TRP in India has been parallel (1991-95)? Star TV was one of the earliest subscribers of INTAM's TRP service, later TAM's, both promoted by advertising, market research and public relations giants globally and they all had come together to exploit the Indian market and engulf India in consumerism. Star's satellite was the vehicle of opportunity.

Star's Six-pronged Strategy

Satellite Television Asian Region (Star) came to India in 1991 as a part of its larger footprint in Central and South Asia, rebroadcasting programmes of a range of other broadcasters including that of the BBC. It was after the entry (1993) of Rupert Murdoch's News Corporation that Star TV emerged with its own India-specific multi-pronged strategy. First, Star took to a local channel, an Indian shoulder to ride on, this was Zee TV.

This included rescheduling some of Doordarshan's top serials and then Pranoy Roy's news channel in English, NDTV, on the Star platform.

The second step was plugging into the cable operating systems to scale up Star's reach far beyond the satellite links that existed then.

Third, Star identified *family values* and *traditions* (take this with a pinch of salt) as the core of Indian society to focus on (for or against) in its content development objective. It, thus, strategically and consciously, took to the popular *soaps* structure for serials and scheduled them with suspense.

Fourth, the Star group recognised the significance of quantifying *number of viewers* that it could claim and count on in a disaggregated and exaggerated way for PR promotion. Star realised early enough that a hook-up with advertisers and advertising agencies was critical to take off, penetrate and for early viability, as the necessary funding would have to come from this sector, so it roped the ad world in.

With four of these above measures working together, Star stormed into India, brave and beautiful. Regressive content helped galvanise its continuity (loyalty) in viewing. Its specially-devised emotion-ridden suspenseful serials on the Indian family, curiosity, glamour and glitter was possible with the support of the best of public relations and advertising support.

Apart from strategies, Murdoch is well known for how to go about dealing with political bosses and lure bureaucrats. Such a strategy paid off and helped Star channels to entrench themselves in Indian families.

Once it took off in India, thanks to TRPs, it was time for the Star TV rocket to come out of tie-ups with Zee TV (and Zee Cinema), NDTV and line up local producers for outsourcing (Balaji etc). Now it acquired the wherewithal and local talent to come up with serials of the themes it had already identified. Star started one channel in Hindi and four in English but all were entertainment channels. Soon it also realised the pulling power music, sports and, of course, cinema had over the subcontinental audience, content suited to the Indian taste for distinguishing in the Indian context.

By 1995-96, within about three years after its entry, Star was able to garner significant advertising revenue constituting 70 per cent of its total revenue. That was how, by 2000, Star could come up with several more channels on its own. How could Star achieve such a feat? Had it seen such success anywhere else in the world? It could do so in India because it could come up with TRP numbers amicably! Without anyone contesting TAM and Star's claims. How many in the public (and even in the academics) knew at that time as to what this TRP was all about? Even Indian channels, including Doordarshan, and advertising agencies which were using Star channels, knew very little about TRPs (except that it was the same system that was in vogue in USA). No one knew how these numbers were arrived at or what was the methodology used and about the meter or people meter, no one had ever seen a picture of any such meter! And, of course, no one, including the government knew how many such metered TV homes were being actually tracked every week. What was TAM's definition of viewership? Or, when one was considered as a viewer? Star TV benefited from all such ambiguities.

Star TV, of course, deserves praise for coming up with the KBC series (2000) in Hindi. It was a well devised serial (although concept wise, it was a copy). This one programme not only raised viewership levels of Star TV to newer heights, it raised advertisement rates too to newer heights. With these episodes, Star TV's viewership edge was made believable and made people forget the kind of hocus-pocus it did with (TRP) numbers in the pre-KBC period.

At the turn of the century, it had already surpassed Zee and Sony in the ratings and was far ahead as the most expensive advertising platform. By April 2001, 34 of the top TRP (rated 50 points) programme were from the Star stable. KBC had put Star Plus as the top ranking channel. According to Star TV's website,[5] in December 2009, Star Plus was the number one Hindi entertainment channel for the previous five years. As many as 42 out of 46 top programmes in India were of Star with over 75 million viewers a week. TAM showed Star retaining its top rank in 2009.

It was in 2008 that the Ministry of Information & Broadcasting sought TRAI scrutiny of ratings as the Ministry had come under fire in Parliament and outside from general public and stakeholders in matters of ratings.[6] These complaints were more about repressive portrayal of women in family serials as soaps continued unabated and continued to be rated as having higher and higher viewership. That there was no self-regulatory mechanism within and among channels or any other independent assessment of any kind in the country further facilitated Star's strategy.

In 1998 Star could start its own news channel, pushing Pranoy Roy's NDTV to lower in the channel ranking. Murdoch himself had to step in to connect with the then Information and Broadcast Minister, CM Ibrahim and the Prime Minister, HD Deve Gowda, to make sure that no Indian media policies come in its way. Much before, at the very outset, Star offered positions to senior functionaries of the Ministry and the Director General of Doordarshan (Basu), and it was obvious to all media watchers, what such allurements meant. By 1992-94, this author had already become aware of the implications of TRPs and was a critique of the methodology. Looking at imported meters from Canada, I had got ECIL[7] to design a viewing monitor meter that was demonstrated in Bangalore and Delhi.

The Hyderabad-based ECIL has designed and manufactured the electronic voting machine and now supplies to a few other countries also. When I met Basu (DG, Doordarshan) and told him why and how Doordarshan was affected by TRPs, and that it/he should take the initiative to support the locally-made and rugged meters that can operate in rural areas also, Basu was not even willing to examine the matter. Instead he lectured me on how I should first go to Mumbai and get it supported by advertisers and ad agencies, instead of Doordarshan taking a proactive view. Finding Basu unconcerned I approached the then Secretary of the Ministry, Bhaskar Gosh, whose pep talk to R Basu made no difference.

BARC: Is it a New Avtar?

Promoted by Indian Broadcasters Foundation (IBF), the Indian Society of Advertisers (ISA) and the Advertising Agencies Association (AAA), BARC (Broadcast Audience Research Council of India)[8] is now offering TV rating service since December 2015. This body has come into being as a result of an initiative of the Ministry in 2008, and specific guidelines from TRAI in 2013. The initial reports of TRAI and the Mitra Committee, and also of the I&B Ministry had come to the conclusion that, apart from the limitation in the sample size and representative character of rating services of TAM, there was a conflict of interest and that such rating should rather be by an independent agency. Both TRAI and Mitra Committee (2010) suggested that an independent agency should be floated by the industry body. It was based on that recommendation that BARC was first registered in 2010. In 2004, the Ministry of I&B entrusted TRAI with regulatory issues in the telecommunications sector and to do with broadcasting license and in 2008 referred viewership rating issue also to it (earlier it was on an ad hoc basis).[9]

IBF[10] was established in 1999 as an apex body of television channels, to promote industry interests. In 2011, IBF had set up the Broadcasting Content Complaints Council (BCCC) with the hope that it helps thwart government intervention, as efforts to regulate the ratings were gaining ground at that time. But at no time until then, did IBF, on its own, take any initiative to address increasing public outcry about TRPs. It was only after the government and TRAI came into the picture that IBF was ready to back the idea of an 'independent rating agency'. The other two bodies, AAA and ISA, are also trade bodies set up to maximise advantage to their members and their respective interests. Their interests are primarily to do with advertising strategies and spending.

Interestingly, in an attempt to scuttle an independent BARC, Kantar (sponsor of TAM in India) had first filed a case in Delhi High Court and questioned BARC's mandate and had started a whispering campaign against BARC. It claimed that its own rating service (TAM) was industry backed, and that industry's self-regulatory initiatives were good enough and as such, there was no need of BARC. At the Ministry's request, as it was under pressure then from public and political parties, TRAI come up with operational modalities in the form of guidelines for rating operations in the country. It was then that IBF, ISA, and AAA came up with a 60:20:20 ratio model of holding in BARC as its promoters. But even after that, TAM persuaded the industry bodies and also BARC to collaborate with it, instead of BARC alone taking to ratings independently. TAM continued with its own 12,000 meters for a while (until mid-2014) and then offered its meters to BARC, floating a formal joint company. That was how BARC could claim 22,000 metered households as the sample for its initial reports in 2015-16. This number is expected to be 50,000 by 2020. Will BARC have 7,000 plus meters yearly, for the next three years? One has to wait and see. Is this a factor for BARC's continued dependence on TAM?

TAM, which had been controlling TV ratings in the country for nearly two decades (1993-2014), cannot be expected to exit quietly. After the Ministry intervened, for the first time in 2008, and earlier, in 2007, after the CMS round table with the I&B Secretary and including a representative of TRAI, TAM tried to expand its sample size and rally support of the industry. Realising that pressure was building up for an independent BARC, TAM tried in different ways to continue as a key player, by being an associate of BARC. With the advantage of sample frames, past data, nearly 12,000 metered TV households, TAM continued its paid for services under a different nomenclature, as some of the subscribers (channels) of ratings were also clients for its other services like advertising monitoring and including TV and radio monitoring and consultancy on related issues. TAM claimed exit from ratings only from February 2016, although it had stopped its weekly ratings earlier. TAM reconciled to its loss only after it entered into a formal understanding with BARC for an arrangement formally by way of a joint company, and in such a way that

TAM could continue to offer its consultancy services in the sector, including to television channels.

BARC is using *impressions* in thousands to mean *viewers*. It is not clear, however, what exactly this implies. Is this the number of times a button is pushed *on* or is there any minimum duration considered for impression, like 60 seconds each time? Although it claims that *impression* implies *reach* and duration or extent of viewing, BARC includes even two-year-olds in the sampled television households (against the earlier four-year-olds being considered *viewer*).

The BARC Board is chaired by the chair of IBF (with 60 per cent stakes in BARC). The Chairman of BARC in 2016-18 was Punit Goenka, Chairman of Zee TV. Its earlier Chairman was Uday Shankar, president of Star TV India. The current Chairman (2018-19) is Nakul Chopra of AAAI. Much earlier, initially KS Sarma, CEO of Prasar Bharati, was its Chairman. Star and Zee chiefs have been the key players of IBF and in that capacity, they are also members of BARC. Although TRAI guidelines indicate that *directors of BARC should not have conflict of interest by virtue of being on the boards of any other television corporations,* the double positions have not become an issue yet. But then, the guideline itself is not practical unless the government itself commits an impressive contribution annually or allows BARC to collect a certain per cent of advertising revenues from television or provide a one-time cost of meters. TRAI should take the initiative to ensure viability and independence of BARC on a continuous basis by looking into its financial provisions.

TRAI and the Ministry, when they initiated the idea of an independent BARC, concluded that there exist conflict of interest in TAM in its relationships and interests in other services, including consultancy service to same media clients to do with contents and ad priorities.

So, *the question today is, how does BARC now explain its arrangement with TAM for an on-going study where TAM's role not so long ago had been of a detrimental nature? Even more, how does it now allow TAM to offer its consultancy services?* MDL (Meteorology Data Pvt Ltd) with 49 per cent share with TAM of Nielsen-Kantar and 51 per cent with BARC, was created to cater to 'joint clients' by both the agencies.

Both, Nielsen and Kantar[11] (partners of TAM) stated that the MDL understanding with BARC 'will keep India as a key market for us'. However, there was no time limit as to how long BARC will rely on TAM-installed meters and the households selected by it. Under the agreement, *TAM has the responsibility for expansion of meters by BARC* in future and that of managing the meters, although the sample plan and maintenance of meters remains that of BARC. No independent expert or viewer representative has been included to guide the affairs of ratings from the board of BARC to counter or balance the critical and continuous role of TAM. How BARC and TAM manage compatibility in the rating service needs to be studied in detail as the service depends on two different makes of meters, two different sample designs being followed, two different sampling frames. The overall impression being given is that 'everything about ratings' is by BARC and as TAM has been a suspect player, now TAM's role is being deliberately underplayed.

BARC, however, has been more transparent than any rating agency in India ever before, with its methodology and operations including arrangements with TAM and other outsourcing arrangements, including for panel recruitment and meter installation given out to Hansa Research, a subsidiary of a top advertising agency. The same agency was also closely associated with TAM earlier. Unlike TAM earlier, BARC started with systematically rotating sample under a 'panel churning policy'.

BARC should be appreciated for its initiative to see that weekly rating impressions are not misused by channels. For this, it has advised channels not to use weekly rating in isolation, 'not to publicise in any competitive context', not to dramatise a week's ratings etc. However, there is no evidence of channels taking cognisance of BARC advice seriously. Some channels continue to hype BARC's figures week after week and in a provocative context and in the same misleading way as before.

Earlier, Uday Shankar,[12] Chief of Star TV, also of IBF (2012), blamed advertisers (and agencies) for making 'bizarre demands' to delay the BARC project. That Shankar was provoked to come out with such a revelation in a media interview indicated a divide.

Week after week BARC has been showing top ten channels and top twenty programmes as per its ratings for urban and rural viewership separately, giving *impressions* in thousands for each.

These ratings have been sampled and analysed for a few weeks. In January and February 2017, for example, Doordarshan does not figure in rural or urban areas, nor do any of its feature programmes top the BARC ratings chart.

Five or six programmes, which figured in the top ten items, were of cricket matches, which were telecast as parts of rights sharing, mandatory for sports transmissions in India. On the other, there was a twice-a-week Doordarshan national serial, *Main Kuch Bhi Kar Sakti Hoon* (MKBKSH) (2016-17), claiming 400 million viewers with 1.4 million

IVRS, becoming India's most-watched television programme. This is an 'entertainment-education' genre programme. And yet, BARC impressions did not reflect this popularity. (See Sharanya Gopinathan's, *How did a DD show on sex education become India's most watched television programme?*)[13] No wonder there were concerns in the Ministry of I&B (April 2018) about BARC ratings 'underreporting viewership numbers for Doordarshan'.[14] BARC ratings for the given period give the impression that there is hardly any difference in the channels' positions that stood out as top ten, despite the sample size being marginally bigger and supposed to be including rural viewers.

Despite knowing well that TRPs influence contents and content priorities of channels all across the nation, TRAI did not take cognisance of this fact at any point, even in formulating its guidelines or thereafter. However, TRAI has rightly observed in its guidelines that 'a flawed TV rating system can hamper the growth of the TV industry' in India. Even BARC did not take any proactive and pre-emptive initiatives in this regard.

In November-December 2016, there were media reports, including on websites and in social media, that some channels, mostly in Telugu, were involved in malafide practice. These reports referred to BARC and the impression was that even after BARC taking over, manipulation was possible and continuing and 30 sting operations were claimed in this exposure. The allegations indicated rates—that is tariff allegedly fixed for different manipulations of rating meter on behalf of different channels—and that some middle men were offering such services. These elements were making presentations to channels on how or what they (outside individuals) do and can be done for higher ratings. The charges for such service/

manipulation were for incentives for watching a channel for certain periods, during certain hours, and for pushing the on button when certain specific programmes were scheduled on a particular channel.

BARC had issued show cause notice to RAJ TV earlier in March 2016 for trying to manage panel homes.[15] BARC reacted to these allegations and even suspended three channels from rating although only for a month (TV 9, V6 and Hindi India News). BARC, of course, is helpless because of the kind of stay that High Courts or other courts give in such cases, preventing BARC from taking action against channels even on coming to know of meter manipulation. Surprisingly, TAM never came up with such issues earlier. It is not known whether any channels were even disqualified or suspended similarly from ratings earlier by TAM. One thing is obvious – that the addresses of TV households with meters are known in the market to unscrupulous elements. BARC CEO, Dasgupta has been quoted saying that 'channels themselves were approaching for information on metered households'. Since BARC and TAM are involved, and the job of installation and meter management is also outsourced to one or two other agencies, perhaps no secrecy could be expected for long.[16] (Also see *Business News*, 'BARC, India's new rating system, proves to be vulnerable to tampering by TV channels just as the earlier TAM was' by Padmaja Shaw.[17])

The speed with which BARC formed an independent three-member disciplinary committee to deal with manipulations, with a retired judge (Judge Mudgal) and representation of the industry and independent experts in measurement technologies, should be appreciated. Such initiatives help restore credibility in ratings. But, in mid-May 2017,[18] when BARC came up with top ratings for the Republic news channel in its very launch week itself, several English channels complained to NBA which included the major ones. They even threatened to exit from the BARC rating system, accusing it of 'distortion', malpractice and unethical practice. These channels included *Times Now TV* and *TV Today*.

The regulator, particularly where the guidelines are set by the regulator, should have the responsibility to periodically review to what extent its guidelines are being followed. Only then does the idea of regulation make a difference. Or, the regulator should entrust the responsibility of review to an altogether independent professional with no conflict of interest and commercial interest, who can periodically do a validation exercise. TRAI lacks any such practice.

TRAI's mandate includes ensuring implementation of licensing conditions as well as guidelines issued by TRAI/ Ministry. TRAI could have tracked why there was so much delay by BARC in coming up with the rating service and what kind of understanding it has with TAM, including in managing meters in the field and also with other outsourced agencies (like Hansa, which undertakes other media studies periodically and also offers its own consultancy to channels).[19]

Even more important for BARC is to go beyond the *reach* aspect, as in the present methodology. There should be efforts to include *actual viewership* aspects and then provide for *impact study* even once in two years as an obligation by channels themselves or by independent professional bodies.

BARC has been in full operation for well over three years now (October 2018). Has BARC made any difference in the content strategies and programming priorities of channels, including the subscribing channels? Because more than three fourth of BARC revenue is from channels, BARC has not been able to offer any argument in that context (November 2017). There is no evidence so far that its *impressions* are any more revealing and reliable than the ratings of the earlier times. The number of subscribing television groups remain 130, having nearly 550 channels between them. Despite this, advertising agencies and advertisers have been the main catalysts of ratings, even though income from advertising amounts to only 20 per cent of BARC's revenue. In fact, it was because of support of IBF's contribution (as of November 2017) and a Rs 145 crore loan of Yes Bank that BARC could keep up with its progress. (That Yes Bank is a major advertiser on Republic TV channel is a different matter). Also, because BARC had increased subscriptions by well over 50 per cent in the last two years, how could BARC have sustained itself without such a loan? Whether BARC is a viable service even after three years needs to be seen, since there are no proposals to ensure credibility of its figures. Although the joint venture between BARC and TAM was for 'meter management', the CEO of BARC, Partho Dasgupta rejected the idea that there existed (in November 2017) any such arrangement on ground. In fact, Dasgupta strongly denied any 'operational link' with TAM (in a meeting on 17 November 2017 in Mumbai).

As an enterprise, rating viewership is unlikely to be viable for the next couple of years, notwithstanding BARC's sincere efforts to do the same ratings better than before. As an independent body, BARC could revamp and reposition beyond meter-based weekly ratings. It could truely boost the power of the Indian subcontinent and be an ally of social change as well. BARC panel of homes as of August 2018 is within 25,000. It is now roping Nielsen India as its 'primary digital measurement partner'. Whether this means involvement of TAM need to be seen.

ORG

The story of Operations Research Group (ORG), Baroda, is not only a story of growth of Indian consumer markets but also of Indian media and its direction. ORG's decline was the beginning of losing sight of direction and the rise of TRPs and the TRP culture. The sudden disappearance of the 50-years-old (1965-2014) ORG from the Indian scene was unceremonious and even mysterious.

What characterises TRP culture? What are the features? Creating artificial competition, taking to a make-believe world with deceptive claims, it is a culture and belief that it is the outcome that matters. There is unconcern for the *impact* aspect; instant glory is all that matters, market and consumer targeting is what TRP culture is all about. Disguising to make people depend on an irrelevant idea and promote it as a benchmark was the modus operandi of the TRP culture. That was how TRP was built up, not over a period of decades but in hardly a couple of years, as if no one ever noticed or understood or as if everyone was mesmerised. The story of ORG was exactly the opposite of that of TRPs in India. That is why we should know about ORG to unravel the TRP regime in India, which has become some kind of a *chakravyuham* where one knows how to get in, not how to get out of a tangle or riddle.

Although Operations Research Group (ORG) started as an

in house support service of the Sarabhai industries in Baroda (now Vadodara), in a matter of couple of years it had risen to become a national think-tank, and fountainhead of market research in India. It was a vision for India's development, a vision of its founder, Vikram Sarabhai, and a mission mode operation of dedicated, confident professionals with no other interest, people like DVN Sarma, S Rajgopal, RC Bhavsar, R Narayana Murthy, Tyagarajan, N Patankar and N Bhaskara Rao. Many were from the Indian Institute of Statistics (IIS), Calcutta.

Started as a retail store audit outfit, ORG become by 1971-73 a household survey research organisation, a first of its kind in India. Although initially focussed on in house products, soon it expanded into a monitor of a range of consumer and household products and later into a research services as well. ORG was the first outside of the government research outfit to have full time field researchers to cover most districts of the country for survey research. That was how it became first a 'large sample' survey agency with 75,000 households in 1971-73 against 500 to 5,000 samples until then. It was acknowledged for its level playing opportunity when it initiated a syndicated service for the first time in the country.

It was endowed with full time staff specialising in a range of subjects. Its infrastructure made ORG a state-of-the research agency. Only three organisations in India had by then acquired powerful third generation computers from Russia. Engineers India and Staff College of India, Hyderabad, were the other two, ORG was the first. ORG's client base included the who-is-who of India's consumer manufacturers, marketers, advertisers, government departments, international agencies including the World Bank. It was ORG which brought to India the phenomena of *growth of brands* and their *proliferation* and *penetration* measurements. Also the *over the counter* pharma formulations.

Media and advertising are two concerns that ORG had although as a natural extension of retail audit and research services. The first National Readership Survey (1970-72) gave big boost to those concerns beyond advertising. This survey first time brought out the idea of stakeholder interests (ad agencies and advertisers), and how such studies could be a win-win opportunity. The first National Family Planning Survey (1971-73), the first ever study on child labour, or even the first ever housing study, were also brought out with dimension for adoption and behavioural change aspects. ORG was already monitoring and analysing advertisement flows into different media and individual outlets first in print media and then radio and cinema and TV channels. With increased interest among advertisers and ad agencies for more data on viewership, it was but natural for ORG to take to these aspects in a holistic way. First, it was recall of programmes seen in the previous week, next it took to diary method where a panel of viewing households record their daily viewing pattern. Based on these diaries and interviews programme preferences were explained. Mere ranking of programmes seen was discouraged for it was argued that ranking could be misleading creative elements and programme preference aspects of people.

My joining ORG in 1972 in a senior position as its Vice President and then as President heading the organisation spreading over two stints first during 1972-75 and then between 1977-89. In between I was with the Ministry of Information and Broadcasting as a special advisor and also had set up research and evaluation capabilities at the Indian

Institute of Mass Communication where I was also a visiting professor. That I declined then the position of director of that Institute was a different matter. During my 15-year period, I scaled up ORG activities but more importantly I foreyed into social development, policy appraisal, public opinion surveys, election studies and entered into futures studies (resulting in India 2021 publication as early as in 1986). Its operations were transparent. That was when based on my experience and on learning that Sarabhais were trying to mobilise capital out of ORG's reputation, I thought such organisations should operate as publicly declared trust or as a society and I insisted that Sarabhais too should pay for the services of ORG. That was when I got into trouble and that eventually led to my leaving ORG. Decline of Sarabhais and its effect on ORG, built as a professional group, brings out why such organisations should be independent. For the sake of a few lakhs Sarabhais handed over the control to someone owning a business magazine who saw the potential and acquired the other reputed Indian market research agency, MARG, and together he handed over to AC Nielsen-all in a matter of less than two years. I refused to join hands with either of them in the 'deals'. Having benefited from the data bases and reputation of ORG among clients, Nielsen dropped the name of ORG within two years.

As a pioneer ORG had set several good practices. Transparency in the research process, not allow conflict of interest, offer level playing opportunity, validation practice of findings for reliability, and that profit not at the cost of objectivity were some of the characteristics of ORG.

On my joining back ORG in 1977 I learned that IMRB had announce the third NRS (it did second NRS but limited to urban) and even collected subscription a year ago from some media houses, it intended to include in the study only those publications which paid a subscription to its reports. Finding all these practices as against fairness practice, I argued that a study called as 'national', without covering rural as ORG did, with the first NRS, and that no such omnibus study could limit coverage to only subscribers, I too announced the third NRS and went to some leaders of the industry like Kasturi of *The Hindu*, RK Swamy of R.K. Swamy, Iyar of Sistas for example, and took them into confidence and went ahead with the field work and completed the study and brought out a separate report for the 'Hindi belt' as the pattern of media growth was distinct and clubbing would not yield practical and region specific insights. That study caused an immediate loss of over fifty lakhs to ORG but credibility and objectivity in ORG was not sacrificed.

A premier publishing house in a state had threatened ORG for showing its competitor daily publication at par in readership and, as a compromise, it offered to sponsor another readership survey in the state. Realising what it meant I took the stand that such a study could be undertaken only after a year, not immediately, as it meant vitiating NRS findings. After a year when the readership study was taken up, that publishing group tried to influence the study by sneaking sample areas from field investigators a couple of days before and distributed newspapers freely to all households and thereby influenced the findings. On my suspecting some such intervention, I called off the study on confirmation of the manipulation. And I returned the advance paid and absorbed the loss and bettered credibility of ORG.

The Advertising Agencies Association (AAA) was against giving findings of NRS in a disaggregated way as it meant change in their functioning and media buying plans. For example, they did not want summative state-wise readership figure for 'English only' and language-wise. For, if that was given the practice hitherto will come under media criticism. For English reader they were spending six times more than what they were for reaching a regional language reader. That exposed their favouritism to English. I presented that by making a presentation of the preliminary findings of NRS to senior information officers of the Ministry. That was how I could contribute to end certain subjective advertising practices until 1973-5. This also meant not 'tailoring' research findings.

ORG initial surveys on television viewership were not so much quantitative exercise, they were more qualitative and not in an isolated way, but occasional sample study on impact or influence on behaviours. For, thousands of studies on TV in USA have established over time effects of TV programmes, and implications of such studies cannot be ignored in any instant ratings of TV viewing. Apart, the television availability in India at that time (1980-90) was limited and viewership was even more so as it was primarily of terrestrial broadcasting, importantly, viewership was uninhibited and composition was overwhelmingly children and women. TV was watched in most cases together by the family. That was why I did not hurry through to commercialise TV viewership studies of ORG. I believed that before becoming public and a syndicated service, such studies should go through wider consultations across the country of different sections of people. The other feature of ORG was that it could bring together advertising trends as it was already tracking and analysing commercial ads in TV channels as in the print media (and for a while in radio and cinema).

Once I left ORG, and on its merger with MARG first and then, with AC Nielsen takeover, it was easy to take on television rating service and consolidate media monitoring activities soon after Nielsen entered the Indian market.

CMS Role in the Context of Ratings

No discussion on TRPs in India could be complete without a special reference to CMS. The 28-year-old CMS (Centre for Media Studies) is an independent not for profit, multi-disciplined research based think tank of a unique standing in India. It has come into being during the critical years of 1989-91 when the country was undergoing a paradigm shift in public policies. The then the President and CEO of Baroda based ORG (Operations Research Group), India's pioneer and large market and media research organisation, N Bhaskara Rao the founder of CMS. After expanding ORG into several new areas of social development, Rao tried to convert it into an independent Foundation. On failing in those efforts, he branched out and positioned CMS as a New Delhi based outfit. In no time CMS acquired national stature with several pioneering research studies to do with social development including environment communication initiatives. Much before, Bhaskara Rao was known for his initiatives in survey research and media studies, including the first 1972 National Readership Survey (NRS). At ORG he initiated television research, advertising monitoring for various media, and impact and evaluation studies. Most of those services AC Nielsen continued to offer having acquired ORG and MARG, the other major Indian market research outfit. Initially Nielsen offered services in the name of 'ORG-Marg', including INTAM TRP Service.

CMS initiatives were based on media studies by Bhaskara Rao in the previous decades (1970-90), specifically studies on reach and impact of media including television. ORG's television viewership monitoring was, with diary, recall and a combination of methods of measuring viewership. It was insights from those various studies and a belief that no such syndicated service could be meaningful without covering rural, CMS had come up with an alternative to meter-based monitoring of viewing. It was felt that the kind of less than 500 first batch of used meters (imported from Canada by a front organisation of AC Nielsen) was deceptive for the Indian scenario. After series of discussion with India's premier electronic R&D company, ECIL, Rao got ECIL to make a meter which was rugged and works in Indian climate zones to monitor viewing. That meter was demonstrated in Bangalore and New Delhi. Based on that he suggested Doordarshan try such meters instead of taking to INTAM service based on a few imported meters at prohibitive cost and in small quantities.

Based on an analysis on the changes in the content priorities of various media, CMS came to the conclusion that the government decision to allow hundred percent FDI into advertising, market research, public relations and media planning has led to devastating effect on the very character of media in India. As early as 1999-2001 CMS had explained the paradigm shift the media of the country was going through. It was explained in an article published first in the *Frontline, Asian Age, Tribune* and *Political & Economic Weekly* (enclosed). One such instrument in that process was TRP. Based on all

"There's good news for those in the ratings game: the Centre for Media Studies (CMS), headed by N. Bhaskara Rao, is coming out with a TV viewership meter by September this year. Evolved by U. Ramakrishna, a Bangalore-based engineer, the device, which looks like a medium sized radio fitted with several buttons, requires the viewer to simply press a button each time he changes the channel. The CMS will make periodic forays into the selected households to collect the floppies". India Today (March 31, 1993).

such background Bhaskara Rao wrote (1993) extensively some of the inadequacies and correctives needed in the meter monitored rating service and brought out that India needed a mix of quantitative and qualitative research based support for television in India. This was the first articles in public media which questioned the methodology and the way the ratings were presented to the public and the way they were being used by channels.

Rao and a senior professor at IIMC, GNS Raghavan, published a book in 1996, *Social Effects of Mass Media* (Gyan, 1996). It indicated the kind of change television viewing had promoted. Based on both the field study and seven workshops CMS held then around the country, this book highlighted the implications of such television programmes on life styles.

As incidents of allegations of tampering or manipulation of meter based ratings started trickle down in 2005, we met the

Minister for Information and Broadcasting, Jaipal Reddy, for a discussion on TRPs and why public criticism was mounting about TRPs. Thereafter CMS worked to bring together the two rating agencies (TAM & a-Map) on a common platform for a presentation and respond to queries in a round table. The meet was attended by the current and immediate past secretaries of the Ministry, representative of TRAI and IBF and several public policy experts. The proceedings of that meet (2007) at India International Centre, New Delhi, were published and shared (enclosed) with a large section of stakeholders. It was after that roundtable and publication of Deliberations, that the government took notice of public concerns and thereafter the Ministry sent out a letter to TRAI asking them to look into rating practices and suggest policy guidelines for rating agencies.

Soon after, in August 2008 itself, TRAI had sent to the Ministry its advise for an independent rating agency and suggested the idea of BARC. TRAI also cautioned about cross-holding and specifically referred to TAM's conflict of interest. TRAI specified in its guidelines (2013) as a part of eligibility criteria that a 'Rating agency should not have in its MOU any activity like consultancy or any such advisory role that can lead to a potential conflict of interest with its main objective of rating'. This was what CMS advocated.

TRAI not only acted without losing time but also made professional advice and its guidelines were elaborate and with foresight. This was what CMS had suggested at the outset to Minister Jaipal Reddy in the 2005 meeting and included in the widely circulated 2007 monograph. CMS role has been not only critical of what and how TRPs were misplaced and misused. However, one point that did not get into the TRAI guidelines was about limitations of meter based monitored ratings and the need for tracking impact or effects of television and the need to study content trends periodically and that all that should be a responsibility of the viewership rating agency. Later in 2013, TRAI also suggested ceiling on commercial time of channels based on CMS research.

Starting with news media articles during 1999-2003 on viewership rating, CMS pursued with roundtable (2007) on ratings after meeting with the concerned Union Minister earlier in 2005. All this led to the Ministry taking interest in ratings in 2008 and requesting TRAI and the appointment of the Mitra Committee (2010). The CMS pursuit was not for exposing TAM, it was for a more responsible, transparent and beyond meter-monitored viewership ratings. It took CMS a decade in all to expose menace of TRPs.

Fudging Ratings!

THE TRPs have been criticised mostly for the very 'small sample' size it depended on. Most in the advertising field justified TRPs on the ground that there was 'no other alternative'. News media which reported TRP did so more often at the instance of public relations corporates who were prompt in putting across an 'interesting news'. They pursued with news media and pushed into news pipeline and news networks, content that suited their goals. Viewers and the public mostly went by cues they received from such media coverage.

From the outset, TRPs were projected as the barometer for *popularity* of channels and programmes. In the initial years, even after five or six years, there was never any criticism of TRP on the basic idea of meter recorded quantification as a surrogate for viewership. Even those who were vocal about size of sample never pointed out that most of the country was not covered in the sample. TAM or INTAM, at the outset and later, never categorically clarified publicly that their ratings were limited to TV households in a few big cities and not representative of the country. And the media, which covered or even hyped TRPs, never corrected their earlier coverage. The weekly TRPs were presented and covered in news media as if they were for the country and reflective of *TV viewing households* at the national level. There was no evidence that even those users of TRP who were allocating crores of rupees of their ad budgets to get these numbers, ever questioned the representativeness of different regions of the country and socio-economic sections of the cities. This itself was a 'scandal' of a gigantic proportion.

A second apprehension about TRPs is about the leak of addresses of TV households with meters, so that manipulation of meter recording is possible, and rating could be meddled with and tampered. This allegation was there in the initial years itself, and it continues even now, after weekly reports started coming under the BARC regime (2016). These allegations come from more than one linguistic region. The impression one gets now is that some people are offering 'this (tampered with) service' at a cost for manipulating the on and off button on the meter at chosen hours in a week or for programmes and for chosen time segments and for certain number of metered households. There is a rate card for every one of these options. This understanding is based on an unauthorised list of addresses of TV households with meter that some middle men or agents have shown TRP subscribers in order to sell their service of manipulating ratings.

A third allegation has been that the households where the meters were installed do not represent the socio-economic category household that is claimed. For example, although institutional viewing was not part of sample frame, meter was installed at some shops or retail outlets in some cities as it was easier to install the meter and also periodic monitoring was possible. Whereas, in the case of households, like for example, upper income households, it may not be easy to install a meter. Since there was never any third-party audit of the lists of sampled households, such apprehensions were never put at rest, not even clarified occasionally.

Yet another aspect never taken into account is the number of meters which had 'actually transmitted data' for the week in context. That is, there will be some metered households where, for one or other reason, meter had not transmitted data, or not even recorded, for that week.[1] This was estimated in one of the earlier years as up to 20 per cent, which is considered a significant number to twist the TRPs for that week. Now, of course, maintenance of meters is outsourced as it is a key function. The reasons for non-function or defective function of a meter could be natural or manipulated as weight-age of every single household is good enough to tilt or change the rating and ranking itself which, in turn, means the value of advertising outlays are at stake.

Connected to this is the apprehension about the number of meters whose data was/is missing week to week. This could be because the meter or the TV set itself had some technical problem, including power failure. All such things obviously affect TRPs. If data from 40 to 50 meters are missed on any week when the sample size is just 4000, for example, the margin of error becomes much higher to the extent of making TRPs guesstimates or misleading. Such information on missing counts was never evaluated and accounted for even for a 5-year period, and never indicated to even subscribers.

The sample size indicated is the number of TV households with meter installed. Of course, everyone in those household is also taken as sample covered and also claimed to be the 'sample population covered'. For example, if some 9,000 meters are installed, the sample claimed is around 45,000 (9,000 x 5 people per household).

Until 2005, TAM covered only one-third of the potential television viewers in the country. As much as 62 per cent of TV homes not covered accounted for 64 per cent of TV viewing time. According to an estimate by ad agency, BBDO in 2003, Doordarshan occupied 31 per cent of total viewership of all TV households in the country. And yet Doordarshan did not figure in TRPs' top ten programmes. This was never explained even when Doordarshan asked for an explanation![2]

In selecting TV household as sample for installing meter implies that metered households are a subset of *active* and *prompted TV households*, not representative of overall TV households even for the respective cities, because TRPs were claimed for metro city-wise also.

The fact was that TV households were included in the sample because they were selected by (an outsourced agency on behalf of) the rating agency for the socio-economic character and for considering to install the meter and also because the household had agreed to maintain confidentiality of the meter in their home. However, these aspects were never indicated while presenting the TRPs even to subscribers. Also pertinent is, what kind of briefing was given to the members of the sample households at the time of installing the meter and the kind of motivation each of them was offered and on what basis or criteria? Another factor to be considered is whether briefing included that the household should see certain duration of the day or certain channels or certain programmes over time? Instances of replacing metered households as most or all members of the household had not seen television at all for days or for not seeing long duration can be found. For example, during summer holidays when all or some members are away for more than a week. Analysts also need to know, when some households were replaced whether they were of the same category (Cable or Satellite) of households in the same demographic category or not is not known as it was not indicated anywhere.

The deceptivity of the TRPs remained a hush-hush talk in close media and advertising circles. It was Zee TV in 2001, which alleged corruption in ratings. Zee claimed that the list of addresses of households with meters were available on sale. The CEO of Zee TV even claimed testing 'how TRP could be fixed' and that 'everything was available at a price'. He even went public with such allegations.[3]

It was obvious that Zee TV had found no logic in TAM ratings putting Star TV and its serials ahead and on the top of the ratings lists as the sample concerned was not at all sufficient to come up with such ranking and ratings, especially as fewer households subscribed to Star TV at the time.

In 2004-05, Aaj Tak channel's *Sabse Tez* news channel, which the India Today group had launched earlier, was expecting to figure on the top of the TRP list as it had the advantage of Aaj Tak's reach and platform. But instead, Star News got the number one TRP slot. An angry Aaj Tak hit back at the rating agency by calling it 'motivated' and having a hidden agenda and said that TRPs 'do not reflect television viewership'. However, neither Zee nor Aaj Tak followed up with any action or reactions (apparently all was sorted out)!

At the height of the TRP regime, Sun TV and ETV too accused the rating agency at one time or other and had even threatened to withdraw from the rating system as they felt their channel and or their programmes were *not getting reflected* in the ratings. Miracle of miracles, soon these channels too had 'sorted out' their differences with the rating agency.

What were the apprehensions of the channels and how did they 'sorted out' or negotiate with TAM was not clear as there was no indication or transparency from either side.

The apprehensions against TRPs were echoed publicly a few years later when NDTV filed a legal case in the USA against the principles of the rating agency, TAM. Why did NDTV file the case in New York? For, NDTV thought that the real people behind TRPs in India were AC Nielsen and Kantar, the two principles of TAM, who were American entities.

Allegations against TRPs continued with more than a couple of channels claiming 'number one' and 'most popular' or 'always No 1' position and simultaneously quoting TAM figures week after week (age group or time segment were given at the bottom of the promotion in such a way that it cannot be read or noticed). This went on not for just weeks but for years. Things were quiet until the Ministry asked TRAI to look into the ratings system.

One of the initiatives BARC took at the outset was to

issue guidelines to subscribers not to mislead the public with promotion of ratings and viewership claims based on ratings. The fact that this notice made no difference to any of the channels and in the way the channels positioned and promoted themselves, is a different matter, a compliance issue that TRAI needs to deal with urgently. TRAI and the Ministry has not so far taken any action against channels blatantly claiming preference viewership's based on misleading TRPs with repeat advertisements week after week.

Conflict of Interest?

A motivating factor for manipulation was the activities of the rating agency. TAM was, at that time engaged in offering 'consultancy services' to the same channels it was rating and certain value-added services to advertising agencies that were advertising on these channels. I raised apprehensions about a 'TRP trap' that channels were falling into in 2001. Ravi Prakash, CEO of Telugu TV9, explained in a seminar (where this author made a presentation) at Hyderabad Centre for Economic and Social Studies (CESS),[4] how the rating agency prescribed 'tips' to his channel to improve ratings by suggesting certain type of coverage (content-wise and the towns). Some other channel spoke about how TRPs were 'guaranteed' by or on behalf of the rating agency. Someone from another channel described TRPs as having a 'tranquillising effect' on channels and their programme priorities. Also, an apprehension was that subscribers to TRPs having multiple channels, who pay higher subscriptions, had differential treatment than those with only one or two channels. Similarity, the channels which were advertisers-heavy enjoyed special advantage in the ratings. The

TRP has led to unnatural competition between channels. It was also revealed that addresses of metered TV households were selectively available to facilitate special programme promotions by certain channels, curtsey one or the other PR agency.

Zee TV or India Today or NDTV were not the first channels to accuse the rating agency of fudging and engaging in manipulation in the process of coming up with ratings week after week. But it was NDTV channel first which demanded a ban on TAM and sought compensation for the damage that TRPs meant and had caused. This was also the first time that the general news media carried stories about NDTV's accusations prominently. Obviously, this was because of the pioneering position NDTV enjoys among news channels. NDTV was also the first channel to take on the principles of TAM (AC Nielsen and Kantar) and file a 198-page suit in a New York Court in 2012. The New York Court (March 2013)[5] struck down the case after hearings on the ground of jurisdiction. The Vice President of NDTV, Narayan Rao, said this in a discussion with this author on 22 February 2017. NDTV accused Nielsen and Kantar of 'Wilful negligence and manipulation of viewership data by TAM and fudging viewer data, causing financial loss, loss of reputation and brand value by releasing incorrect viewership'. NDTV claimed damage of one billion dollars.[6]

NDTV accused Nielsen-Kantar of adversely affecting its revenues, reputation, brand value and for 'recklessly disregarding any responsibility'. The accusation of NDTV meant that TAM- promoted ratings had suppressed full play of Indian genius for, contents of some NDTV channel were of a different model than what TAM promoted.

In December 2016, the *Mint* daily carried a news story of alleged tampering of rating by manipulating use of TV in metered TV households.[7] A more detailed news story, which was widely talked about was Professor Padmaja Shaw's article in *Hoot*, a leading web magazine.[8] 'BARC India's new rating system proves to be vulnerable to tampering by TV households, just as the earlier TAM was', the story screamed. She referred to 30 sting operations on how the meter was manipulated, with some details. This explosive article is reproduced here. In the wake of this expose, BARC suspended only three channels, that too for only for four weeks. It could not take on more channels as a Hyderabad Court had restrained any such punitive action.[9]

Had the rating agency (TAM) been told to bring to the atten of the concerned public all cases of anomalies and manipulations to their notice, such manipulations could have been avoided much earlier.[10] On the contrary, certain disregard was alleged, including by NDTV. What is equally curious was that Doordarshan despite being the worst effected channel, neither Prasar Bharati nor the I&B Ministry were concerned or ready to do something about it. It was also this author's proactive meeting with the then Minister that made the Prasar Bharati CEO to call a senior AC Nielsen functionary from Singapore to a meeting in which this author too was invited.

BARC's insensitivity to competitive compulsions became obvious when it showed the just-launched Republic channel on top of the ratings with 53 per cent 'viewership' (instead of *impressions*) for the very first week of launch.[11] All other English news channels noted this as a result of 'distortion', malpractice and manipulation of the new ratings service. In fact, News Broadcasters Association (NBA)[12] went to the extent of issuing a public statement, accusing BARC of releasing 'inflated and corrupt data for Republic TV'.

India Today even threatened to exit from BARC ratings and it's Council. This case brought back the old suspicions and revived doubts about independence of the new agency offering the ratings (BARC). The Republic channel had taken competition to new height (or to a low level) by prominently advertising ratings and repeatedly in a day. BARC should be appreciated for constituting a three-members committee with Judge Mudgal and an expert, Paritosh Joshi, to go into the allegations and accusations of misuse and manipulation of TRPs. But nothing further has been heard about the deliberations of this committee (2018).

Telugu 360 sting exposes TV ratings manipulation

BARC India's new ratings system proves to be vulnerable to tampering by TV channels just as the earlier TAM was.

—*PADMAJA SHAW* reports

A TV grab from Telugu 360's sting operation

The website, Telugu 360, has broken open the ratings controversy that has been "brewing around" the suspected manipulation of viewership numbers by various channels in the Telugu market. It has conducted 30 sting operations with various individuals who were tasked with the management of metered households for BARC India.

The agents involved in this, according to Telugu 360, approach the Broadcast Audience Rating Council (BARC) personnel installing the meters and get details of households selected. It is not clear from the videos uploaded whether BARC India has subcontracted the management of households to these local agents, or if it is a simple case of leaked information.

The agents then visit the households and convince them to watch the channels they are promoting for a fee. Each of the agents has said on camera that they have some 15 to 20 households under their 'control' and can get them to watch news channels for a fee of 1000 rupees and entertainment channels for 2500 rupees. If the agent 'manages' viewers for 4 news channels and 2 entertainment channels, then he will earn 1,30,000 rupees for 15 households and 1,80,000 for 20 households.

Channels bear these costs of 'managing' the willing households fitted with meters. They also directly call the households and verify if viewership is actually happening on the ground.

"Channels bear these costs of 'managing' the willing households fitted with meters".

The agents tutor the men and women in the compliant homes to tune in discreetly, clocking two hours per channel in various day-parts, so that the patterns of viewing do not give rise to suspicion. They also tutor them on how to answer the BARC

India inspection teams when they come to check.

It is obvious from the sting footage that all the participants in the deal know that this is fraudulent and that they are playing along for money. Some women have also said that channel personnel call to check if they are watching as per requirement, as well. From the video footage it appears, the reporter has pretended to be the representative of a channel who has come to negotiate with the agents and the viewers.

In the videos uploaded so far, some 10 major Telugu entertainment and news channels have been mentioned the website has uploaded the details of the personnel indulging in this along with the videos of them describing the modus operandi.

Broadcast Audience Ratings Council India has barred the reporting of ratings of two Telugu channels, TV9 and V6 along with India News, "from week 46 to 49 of 2016 due to suspected malpractices". India news got a stay from the Bombay High Court, and V6 and TV9 have approached the court. The sting comes close on the heels of these developments.

As far back as in February this year, BARC India CEO Partho Dasgupta revealed that BARC India people are being approached by channels for information about metered households.

The battle to corner the 181 billion rupee advertising pie at stake in the Indian television market has been raging across the country and has manifested in the over-crowded Telugu market in more virulent ways.

Some months ago, a senior management person of Sakshi TV complained that the day-wise ratings of ETV (week 36 to 41, saw an increase of 294%) and ABN-Andhrajyothi (week 32 to 41, saw an increase of 302%) were suddenly spiking upwards, without any major event or change in programming to account for it.

"Do we see the disciplinary action as a positive step or do we say that the system appears to have lost its credibility comprehensively"?

Similar unexplained wild fluctuations were observed in other cases and the complaints reached BARC, who apparently were unable to secure the ratings process from manipulation. However, with the reporting of some channels' ratings finally banned, and with the names of several other channels coming out in the sting, it is unclear how this is to be understood. Do we see the disciplinary action as a positive step or do we say that the system appears to have lost its credibility comprehensively? With the issue now in court, it is to be seen how this high stakes game will end.

When the BARC system began, there was much hope resting on it as it is run by three major industry bodies, the Advertising Agencies Association of India, the Indian Society of Advertisers, and Indian Broadcasting Foundation, under the guidelines of the information and Broadcasting Ministry. None of the agencies is allowed to hold more than 10% stake in its ownership.

The earlier system under TAM were covering 225 towns, comprising 9100 homes and 40,000+ individuals from January 2013 (as quoted in the TRAI consultation Paper on Guidelines/ Accreditation Mechanism for Television Rating Agencies in India dated 17 April 2013).

Unlike the Tam system, BARC India has increased its sample size to 20,000 households, with a provision to increase it to 50,000, gradually by adding 10,000 each year. It has also included a rural sample and has put in place a new socio-economic category (SEC) based on the education of the primary breadwinner of the family and asset ownership from a set of 11 asset categories.

The programmes are watermarked on the audio track of the 427 participating channels and weekly sweeps of ratings data are generated from the BAR-O-meters set up at statistically chosen sample households.

BARC set up a network of managers to maintain the meters and to train the recruited viewer-households. This then appears to have become the weak link, with these individuals themselves becoming complicit in manipulating the system for fairly small sums of extra money.

Often one hears loud proclamations of self-regulation from the media industry. BARC India is a body controlled and run by the three respected industry associations. Some of the member channels are working full time to undermine all efforts at evolving a credible system of ratings, primarily because they have entered a crowded, unsustainable market, and appear to see no fair way of dealing with competition.

The viewer's real reactions or preferences are also being betrayed in this process of manipulation. Ravish Kumar of NDTV India in an impassioned address was seen asking the audience why they watch television news when it is no longer news. Perhaps, those who manage ratings have an answer to this.

The only silver lining in this sordid saga is perhaps the fact that not enough members of audiences are watching the unappetising mess dished out to them and the channels are finding other means to snare advertising rupees. It is reassuring to know that the audience are steadfastly refusing to dumb down!

(Source: The Hoot)

Beyond a TRP Scenario

THE SOONER the 'Days of the TRP' are over, the better for the television of the country. Can we erase myths that ruled India's television scenario for nearly three decades without demolishing the euphoria around TRPs? It may be difficult to erase in a year or two the use of and belief in TRPs but people in advertising and media, who perpetuated a TRP regime and are expected to be rational and evidence-based professionals, can demolish the TRP culture if only they are determined.

Theoretically, advertising professionals, if they can be logically convinced, should be the first ones to go for an alternative. But when elements of self-interest are involved, no such argument makes much headway unless concerted efforts are made together with the channels. Channels need to be convinced of how misleading the ratings methodology has been and what they have missed. They missed much more than what some channels benefited from the TRPs. Advertising entrepreneurs and practitioners need to realise that first. They should realise that their future is far more challenging than a week to week outlook of their prospects. They should realise that immediate growth in market shares is temporary, same way as politician's opportunities during elections are. Mere replacement of the rating agency after denigrating its reliability and its service, with almost the same methodology and continuing with the same field operations, is not a departure from what has been, especially since TAM is a partner or outsourced agency with the new agency (BARC). No doubt, its association with TAM has endangered BARC's credibility.

In the wake of the first NRS (1972-75), I had engaged with advertising agencies and advertisers and supported their endeavours to find rational ways for budgets and outlays for various media campaigns. They were then constantly in search for optimising input and output ratios. That was how the first (1974) media planning model (by Subroto Sengupta, a faculty at IIM-A) was viewed as a big breakthrough and helped media planning departments of advertising agencies emerge as specialised units and even as profit centres.

Almost twenty years later, the advertising community embraced TRPs of television, TV becoming an instrument for expanding and penetrating into markets and reach audiences. Advertising professionals are dynamic, and in search of logics both for creative strategies and media plans and prefer quantitative formula (to convince their clients – advertisers). TRP came handy for them in that process and initially boosted media planning functions.

But now, it is time to think beyond, for the next level, with a new combination of new media and thrills of digitalisation and broadband. TRP is two decades old. The meter monitoring no longer holds good with people watching television programmes on smartphones. If 2020 has to be a take-off year with newer challenges for growth beyond, it is time to think of formulas which encompass much beyond immediate compulsions and beyond such aspects as ratings on a weekly and daily basis.

The analytics era is already on the anvil and should guide the advertising community to think very differently and much beyond TRP-centric rating and ranking. It is good that BARC is structured as a not-for-profit set up (unlike profit motivated private limited companies, as it is in the case of TAM).

I remember when I brought out a separate report for the 'Hindi belt' out of the third NRS in 1978-79, prospects for media growth comparing the trend in the previous decade, it was obvious that growth opportunities in these States were much higher than what was realised by then (by media owners and advertisers). In the same way, it is high time now that advertising entrepreneurs realise that what they had accomplished with TRP was much less than the opportunities that lay ahead. That is why they now need to chase a new formula and new models that help take new and higher growth paths and also make an overall impact.

Similarly, television channels too need to realise that they are yet to unleash their potential and the growth, whatever they had so far, was far less than the opportunities.

TRP was a hyped and over-used idea. It no longer commands credibility, nor does it reflect reliability as more and more people know of the futility of ratings and the emptiness or superficiality of weekly ratings. Some kind of saturation had already set in by 2010. That TRP does not correctly denote viewership as was claimed in the earlier years is now widely known.

BARC had started using the word 'impressions' to express meter-recorded data. However, What BARC means by that and when does it or whom does it consider as an *impression* is not substantiated. And it hurt its own credibility when it called Republic TV's TRP as *viewership* rating. *Impression* could also be described as *reach* in thousands (as before). This *reach* could be of a channel, of a feature programme or a commercial or of a time slot. If that is what BARC means by *impression,* then that should be obvious.

Reach was what we used initially as the primary data from the field. It was after an analysis that criteria for reader, viewer and listener were arrived at, based on the extent of exposure which varied in the case of each media. In the case of print media, for example, the one who had *read* (*recalled*) a newspaper 'at least two or three times a week' was described as a *reader*. In the case of television and radio, it was the number of times in a week one had (*recalled*) *seen* or *heard* and this was considered as a *viewer* or a *listener* and the same was presented in three grades. BARC needs to explain clearly, what is an *impression* and when is it *active* and when is it *casual*?

BARC's *impression* service, in place of TAM's TRPs, is not a durable idea – but BARC offers a hope. It should revamp itself and come out of TAM's model and framework, with a far more comprehensive methodology in order to reposition the 'rating' idea and its relevance in the new media-television scenario.

TRAI should facilitate this process with additional guidelines in such a way that interests of viewers and impact aspects are taken in. The Ministry should support BARC without impinging upon its character. BARC can gear up to avail new challenges and opportunities with a three-year perspective plan (2021).

But the new methodology should go beyond *reach* and into *exposure* and note the behavioural aspects as well. Also, it should be realised that it is a waste of resources to ascertain *reach* week after week. No wonder the News Broadcasters Association had suggested a monthly report (in place of a weekly). In the case of television, the *behavioural* and *implication* aspect, is far more relevant for the country. *Reach* is good enough for immediate or instant outcome. For advertisers, *exposure* is far more pertinent for an evaluating model. There is need for clarity on those aspects, which in turn determines the methodology.

Sample Size, Socio-Economic Character

Regarding *sample size* and *representativeness* there are two aspects. First, there is limitation. Not any or every TV household shortlisted for selection agrees to install (attach) a meter to the TV in their household. This limits the representative character of the sample. Then, of course, it is not merely the size of the sample but how well it represents the universe of the households with a television set. As such, it matters how well the sample selected is spread (instead of concentration in any one pocket or cluster) and of course, the procedure followed for selecting the shortlisted TV households. One has to agree to install the meter and allow the meter to be checked as and when required by a representative and, more importantly, agree to push the on button and also the off button by everyone in the household, every time family members come in front of the TV or are within its radius.

Not everyone having a TV is likely to agree to these terms and conditions even after gifts and incentive are provided for agreeing to install and operate the on-off buttons on the meter or its remote by every member of the household. To this extent, it cannot be said that such a *sample of TRP* is representative of the universe of 'TV households'.

I remember when we were trying to set up a panel of TV households (1989-90), households in higher socio-economic category were not forthcoming and were reluctant to be part of any such 'panel'. In the case of installing a meter (without knowing its architecture), even a much higher percent of households in that category will be reluctant to allow any such meter installed in their home. Then the question of confidentiality. No wonder there were allegations initially that households where meters were installed did not belong to the category that it was supposed to, as per the sample plan indicated or claimed by TAM. Selection procedure is as important as the size of the sample.

TRAI and the Ministry were expecting that BARC will have 50,000 metered TV households by 2020, reasonably representing the TV households in the country, including rural. In 2016, BARC claimed 22,000 samples, including 10,000 (or 12,000?) metered households of TAM (as of 2013). Given an opportunity to add around 25,000 TV households to the sample, BARC should explore to cover and reflect the viewing pattern of non-metered TV household segments. There could be a sub sample of such a panel of households. This would also help represent rural India a little better. That enables far more representative sample frame. The coverage of non-metered TV households could be by phone or/and personal interviews with members in TV households. In fact, a sub sample of phone or personal interviews could be both with metered and non-metered households. BARC shows that it had 33,000 households with meter (as of November 2017). BARC should focus on reaching 50,000 households with meters rather than getting sample numbers by counting every one (including the 2 years old) in the sample size.

IVR (Interactive Voice Response) method of instant feedback being a trend now in some services of governance and customer servicing, IVR can be integrated into an audience research methodology as well. There could be a sub sample based on IVR.

As TAM earlier, BARC too is assuming that every member (of 2+ years, earlier 4+) of the household is participating in the pushing 'on and off' of the buttons every time during a day a television programme is seen. And, 2 to 7 years old children could be grouped as a separate category of viewers.

This aspect needs consultations with teachers, parents and social activists. Some rethink about both recording and analysis aspect with regards to children of 2 to 7 years age group will sharpen the findings and the exercise becomes more sensitive.

It is time to revisit the suggestion of a monthly report, instead of weekly as at present. A few years ago this suggestion by Justice AP Shah of the News Broadcasters Association was rejected by advertising agencies.[1] As many as 25 ad agencies even threatened to withdraw from subscribing to BARC rating if the report is not weekly. It should be possible to distinguish the short-term needs of advertising agencies from that of long-term ones.

Also, BARC should bring out weekly and monthly reports on an experimental basis, going by response pattern of households with a cut-off percent. That is, households where the response rate of some operating meters during the week is less than two hours (for example), they should be included in a monthly report. This is likely to indicate the reliability of even the weekly report. And this helps drop households or reconsider households with low response rate.

The idea of a 'meter maintenance group' which BARC had setup is good, but this is a sensitive issue and interaction of people of this maintenance group with meter-households has to be done very cautiously.

BARC should reposition itself as an independent rating and television research agency while continuing with its present promoters. TRAI should recommend to the Ministry to give an annual grant or and give one-time seed money for procuring and installing meters. BARC should not be under the control and obligation of IBF, ISA and AAA for ever. But they should remain as promoters and key players. BARC should become a viable proposition by 2022 and have an independent chair by 2020 (not ex-officio IBF), with no stakes in television and media concerns.

The Ministry should ensure that IBF, ISA and AAA fulfil their obligations with prompt payment of commitments. Support to BARC should not be in doubt or uncertainty. A certain percent of advertising outlays or any revenue accruing to government from out of television advertising in the country should be allocated for viewer-centric and basic research, including ratings.

Parallely, BARC should explore with high tech agencies like ECIL, TCS, Infosys etc for the next level of technology to replace both peoples meter and its own Bar o meter, with accuracy on recording family members' exposure to television and for transmitting and analysis of the data in a disaggregated and composite way. Also, it should seek advice of someone like Nandan Nilekhani or Kiran Karnik on the level of technology and explore a two-way communication with sampled households. A sociologist or anthropologist or a social researcher from academics should be inducted into the BARC board. BARC should take special initiatives to better transparency in its operations and methodology. Of course, it has already taken measures in that direction. Unlike in the previous years, it should hold at least one 'validation conference' with subscribers of its services annually and another one with 'active users' of its data like academics and independent research institutions like ASCI, CSDS, CMS etc.

Chip in TV Set Top Box

Almost a decade after the Ministry of I&B took the initiative to look into television viewership ratings, it has decided to have a 'relook' for 'more accurate viewership data' by incorporating a chip in the set top box. Why did the Ministry suddenly take to this initiative in 2018? Has the Ministry reviewed the on-going viewership monitoring arrangement by BARC?

Four reasons were informally indicated to the news media. First, there is a 'monopoly' in viewership data (although this is not exactly so). Second, the methodology is not transparent (BARC has a better system than its predecessor). Third, the belief that a chip captures viewership of channels more accurately as all DTH households will be covered. There were also concerns in the Ministry that BARC, like its predecessor TAM, is not reflecting Doordarshan's viewership. Fourth, the Ministry apparently wants to use viewership data for 'strategising' its own communication campaigns. In other words, it will mean, for communicating the government's and therefore, the ruling party's, strategies, especially keeping the forthcoming general elections in view.

However, there are no indications that the Ministry or even Prasar Bharati or Doordarshan ever conducted an assessment of BARC's rating operations or advised it with any connectives for accuracy or reliability or representativeness. And there is no other exercise on rating operations other than CMS's which had conducted an independent review of viewership ratings some time ago.

All that apart, this idea of a chip in set top boxes of DTH households is not a one-shot affair. This means recalling set top boxes for fixing the chip, assuming that DTH operators agree for such an arrangement. The Ministry approached TRAI in 2018 for advising the concerned stakeholders accordingly. TRAI should be appreciated for advising the Ministry to make such a reference to the Regulator formally, so that TRAI is empowered to take such a measure as a part of the licensing condition to DTH operators.[2]

If the Ministry pursues its plans of a chip in set top boxes for viewership data of DTH households, it obviously destabilises BARC rating operations and even makes BARC an unviable enterprise.

Even more, the Ministry will be sparking a new controversy involving privacy of TV households in the name of viewership ratings. It is very unfortunate that an otherwise well-informed ruling party Member of Parliament, Subramanyian Swami has attributed 'fake news (read anti-Hindu news)'as due to 'cronyism of BARC-like freelancers'.[3] Are we trying to benefit from Facebook experiences instead of avoiding embarrassing controversies?

One thing is for sure – this is as good a time as ever to take a substantial review of viewership rating practices, rather than trying to create an altogether new controversy! Now is the right time to *get out of instant viewership measurement and go for a qualitative assessment approach,* keeping the *implications* and *impact* aspects more as a priority but get the study conducted independently, professionally and transparently.

There is a 'rethink' and the desire to 'reposition' TRP on the part of the some channels. This is evident not only in the case of channels who had alleged fraud on the part of TAM's ratings but even the ones which benefited, like the ten year old Viacom 18 Media.[4] *Colors* (2008) is one of its 42 channels including in regional languages, some of the others are MTV, NICK, VHI. Viacom is in five different kinds of media business. It now claims 'distinctive identity', 'strong focus on engaging' and describes itself as 'an agent of change', thinks to 'redefining entertainment' and also claims 'supporting women's empowerment' to become an agent of an 'agent of change'. It is a much-desired reposition. Such a realisation across channels goes a long way in retrieving television to its pride of place in India.

BARC's agreement with outsourced agencies, including TAM, requires to be reviewed. Three aspects need to be far more objective. First, TAM should not have even a remote hold or role in any rating operations, especially in BARC. TAM should not have any future association without a time bar indicated. Equally important, no one associated with BARC should be engaged in conflict of interest roles or engaged in cross media businesses, even engaged in any 'consultancy' with television channels.

BARC should confine itself to uphold the spirit and provisions of 2013-2014 guidelines of the Ministry as recommended by TRAI. Its dependence on advertisers and channels should be on the decline because of the increasing subscription and credibility of its ratings. TAM ratings have made television channels depend more than ever on advertising. If subscribers of BARC rating services do not confine or limit the use of that to a weekly assessment which affects the very credibility of the ratings, BARC has a chance to be neutral. Even more, the very credibility of channels themselves, are under threat if they compromise BARC. Channels need to be convinced how 'independently and transparently conducted ratings' can help them as much, even to better their viability aspect. BARC should not hesitate to use the 'shame and shine' practices of channels when they violate guidelines.

There is no doubt that television is a family medium, even more so in India. The households with more than one TV set are insignificant as of now. The 'people meter' needs to be looked at again and just claiming a larger sample (including all members in the household), is more a PR move to cover up the 'size of sample', even for BARC. Nevertheless, obtaining viewership of children, women and certain sections of people in a household is important and should be part of the rating methodology more distinctly. But the methods cannot be uniform for children and others.

The Way Forward

Now that there is certain realisation that mere 'looking at the screen of the television' by itself may not mean much for introducing specific content by channels, it is time to review the very idea of the meter-based ranking and rating, the structure of meter being what it is.

It is time for the next generation meter to capture active viewership. The rating idea and methodology over the last two decades was based on what interests advertisers and ad agencies more, it projected viewership in such a limited way that channels determine or mould programmes palatable to a specific segment of viewers and have promotion value for products, brands and services of advertisers and other agencies. The objective was not so much to get the best out of television for the country or for a win-win situation for stakeholders, which includes viewers and the people of the country.[5]

Vikram Sarabhai and people of that generation thought of television as a tool for empowering people, supportive of national development, enriching children and fulfilment of national goals. Towards that ultimate purpose, all those engaged in contributing or determining the priorities of television today should take a retrospective view and chalk out a way forward plan and strategies for a more inclusive and concerned television.

Content strategies and priorities of television channels in India should not be limited to or ratings-driven. Nor should they be advertising driven. Advertising support, of course, is unassailable and will remain sought after. Rating without *impact* or *implications* aspect taken into account and consideration could be misleading. This requires that ratings do not meddle or interfere with creativities and even not come in the way of innovative initiatives of channels, including scheduling plans. Any rating service should help promote creativity and original programming as much. Dependence of channels on advertising or/and advertising-centric contents should not be forever. Creative programming and content strategies including time schedules should, of course, help viability of channels as well. That was what I contended in 1995 when I brought out the *Mass Media and Marketing Communication Perspectives in 2020.* [6]

Television in general and some contents of channels in particular will have impact on non-viewers as well. How can that be captured and get reflected? Of course, the size of this non-viewer segment keeps changing from time to time. This is what is known as the 'diffusion effect' of channel contents or some specific programmes, including news bulletins and some current affairs programmes. Channels are expected to capture and win over such people as viewers and active viewers. Ratings should help reflect such a migration process as well.

Research on viewership of television channels and its *impact* and any evaluative assessment should be independent of advertising and even of the broadcasters. For such an ideal scenario, the state should provide annual funding linked to specific research tasks periodically, even once in five years is desirable. This funding could be fully or partly by the government, based on the number of TV sets in operation or certain percent of advertising outlays or on the basis of population covered by TV. The kind of rating and research service should be specified so that the independence allows certain rounds of ratings in a year to bring out impact on children and education, women and the poor over a 5 or 10 year period, for example. And reports of such research should be in the public preview or access. Transparency in the process should be obvious.

Restraints & Responsibilities

Best of television is possible when certain restraints and responsibilities are taken at five different levels. Ratings makes sense only when such a responsible system is in place and evident. First, self-regulation restraint by individual channels. HMTV was the first news channel in Telugu a few years ago (2012) to institute an independent 'watchdog' or 'overseer' where periodically, an internal review of contents of the channel is conducted with the help of an independent and credible personality. Even NDTV announced Veteran Luminary Fali Nariman as its ombudsman in 2017. A forum should be operational for redressal of complaints of viewers. Channels individually should showcase such efforts even in a suo-motto way. Details of the concerned ombudsman should be in the public domain.

Second, citizen or viewer activism is the best bet any time. Without active viewer, no television channel can be moderated, become responsible and a social institution. The least a viewer can do is write back to the channels what they would like to see individually and as a family. They should be prepared to boycott a programme or a channel when things go overboard and even appreciate when special initiatives are taken by a channel or a programme. Members in panel households should be sensitive about what ratings mean and what the general public should know about the reliability of the ratings and how their preferences can be conveyed.

Third, channels should organise into associations, not only to fight business interests as they are, but also take proactive initiatives, deliberate on contents trends and bring in content concern on their own instead of depending on ratings. Of course, channels being diverse in their origin and interests, cannot be expected to come together always.

Both, the Press Council of India and the Law Commission do not think such arrangement by such associations in vogue so far have made much difference. Nevertheless, such efforts have to be on-going and no big difference can be expected in one go or in an immediate time frame, considering that TRP has been in control for twentyfive years now.

Fourth, there should be an independent regulator with legal backup. But this ought to come into the picture only if other measures in a given context have not consistently worked. A regulator should not be part of the government or a Ministry. This system should come into picture only on a complaint and after exploring other ways to resolve issues. A suo-motto provision should be there.

Fifth, academic and other professional groups must act on their own with their own methodology to see that television channels function with moderation and with certain concerns for the interest of people of the country. They should bring out the specifies as and when channels or programmes offend viewer sensitivities.

The government of the day should come into the picture as a last option and only if it is essential in any given situation. But the government or the agency responsible for the initial clearance of the channel should at least have a few minimum obligatory conditions like annual declaration on shareholding, content focus and responsibilities and desirability of feedback assessment of *impact* aspects. That is, channels should indicate as part of their annual declaration any public outcry or complaints on any content, schedule of programmes and also indicate suo-motto any 'conflict of interest'.

Media establishments or enterprises should come under the transparency regime in their own interest and avail the practice of sharing with the public their operation processes. Only in such a scenario, does the idea of rating on a daily or weekly basis makes sense and enhances its potential for a 'better' TV operation.

Channels should encourage independent watchdogs and promote feedback and viewer interactive mechanisms and avenues. Eventually, this component should acquire much higher significance in the overall matter of content priorities.

TRAI should take up promotion of voluntary regulatory concepts and this should not be viewed as responsibility of any one agency. Measures like 'write back' among TV viewers should acquire seriousness and such a culture acquires ground, once channels respond back. The 'Talk-back' culture is possible only when channels take the initiative, as some of them had already started welcoming complaints some time ago.

It should be obligatory on the part of BARC to take up specific studies on the *social impact* aspects of TV channels periodically. The impact of programmes shown as standing high on ratings week after week should be assessed.

What *impact* the rating of programmes have had and difference such ratings have made to programmes and viewership's over a three-year period and how has rating changed programme priorities and caused band-wagoning too should be tracked. The copycatting phenomena among channels should be studied, preferably by academics. BARC should assist such studies. Such studies in the context of women and children in particular should be viewed as obligatory on the part of the rating agency.

At the 2007 CMS round-table meet where the two rating agencies (TAM and a-map) made a presentation of their systems raised several questions which CMS highlighted for larger public attention. These issues raised at that time are worth recalling at a time when the agency has changed. These posers raised at that time in 2007 are appended here as many of them are pertinent even now in 2018 for BARC as well.

The idea of 'awards' to channels, programmes and creative initiatives offer reliable feedback and insights. If it is based on certain objective criteria, if the process is transparent and stakeholders are involved in critical decisions, only then do such awards hold meaning. Periodic awards, together with 'ratings' should reflect certain concerns and directions for future course of channels and television in India. Awards should not be for band-wagoning. The awards should happen at three levels – as an internal exercise by a channel or a network for its own programmes and priorities (as some channels are already doing); by independent organisations, not in conflict of interest with channels or television. Third, awards could be by a business enterprises. TV awards are in vogue in India for nearly a decade. Have they made any difference in any respect? Have they led to any experiment or a deviant initiative by any channel? Awards should contribute for overall standards in the industry and help bring transparency. If over one-third of awards are for crime-centric programmes and more of the same, then what difference can such an award make? Awards should stand-out for bringing new insights and course correctives, not in echoing TRPs or as a PR for channels. Awards should help channels and producers pause and relook at what difference they have made and can make now and help them reposition for making a difference.

Regulator (TRAI) should be concerned to see whether its suggestions and recommendations, as in the case of ratings, are being implemented and followed by BARC, channels and even the government.

The channels-dominated mass media scenario in India requires certain 'safeguards' as an obligation of channels for certain rights of viewer and people at the viewing end, particularly about effects, immediate and delayed and linkages in that process.

Since not all viewers in meter households are normal or natural or interested viewers, the viewership should distinguish *casual* or *passive* and 'active' viewers. This may amount to differentiate 'reach' and 'exposure' of a channel or a programme or a time chunk.

It is time to revisit the landmark 1995 Supreme Court Judgement[7] that said 'airwaves are public'. The judgement implied that airwaves cannot be used for private interests without obligations, transparency and coming under an independent regulator. "Public interest" provision should apply to all channels, broadcasters, public and private. Ratings cannot make that concern redundant at any point.

Annexures

The seven papers enclosed together present an overview of the issue in context. The unfolding issue of ratings was indicated first in 2001 in general and more specifically later in 2005. That is five years after ratings had taken off and taking roots. It was after these writings that a movement against TRPs gained ground and picked up. Then came a time when the government could no longer ignore the rating controversy. That was when Amit Mitra, of FICCI, was made to look into and come up with a perspective and, simultaneously, TRAI was formally entrusted with this contentious rating issue.

Of Contents & Control, N Bhaskara Rao, *Frontline* 2001
The TV TR(A)P, N Bhaskara Rao, *Asian Age*, 2001
Television Viewership Measurement: Dilemma and Changes: CMS Round Table, New Delhi, March 2007
Preface to Monograph by P N Vasanti
Summing up: Some Posers on TV Viewership Ratings

Frontline, September 14, 2001
Media "Of Content and Control"
N. Bhaskara Rao

When the path and pace of the media in India are by and large set by advertising and market research, which are often controlled by foreign corporate, any debate on the entry of foreign capital into the print media may be irrelevant.

The Indian media scene has gone through a dramatic shift in recent times both in terms of content and control. While media content is more and more market-driven, control has now shifted, although indirectly, to "foreign corporate". And yet out political masters continue to revive irrelevant debates such as the 1995 Cabinet decision against the entry of foreign capital into the Indian print media, when in fact the "foreign factor" is already "moderating" the priorities of most media in the country. The debate on foreign equity is perhaps meant to side-line the core of the issue-the direction of the Indian media.

Today advertising and market research, in many ways, determine the scope of the media. Both these functions are in the hands of corporate controlled by foreign corporate. Let us examine this phenomenon, which we could either brush aside as a "global trend" or get down to understanding the larger implications. The path and the pace of the media today are set as much by advertising, market research and media planning as much by ownership.patterns and journalistic trends. The control of these "determining factor" has, by and large, slipped out of Indian hands with no one making an issue of it.

First, the share of advertising in the total revenue of the media has been on the increase, from a "supplementary" 25 to 30 per cent some decades ago to a "supportive" 45 to 55 per cent today. In fact, in the case of television channels advertising has been a "primary source" (50 to 70 per cent) to sustain themselves and to the extent of "determining" their priorities and preoccupations. Even in the case of some big newspapers, revenue from advertising constitutes 60 per cent of the total revenue. The recent media boom in India is often attributed to advertising. That is, advertising today sustains and steers the media.

Secondly, advertising in newspapers and on television today is mostly by multinationals and big corporate. In fact, the top 15 advertisers account for three – fourths of the advertising revenue of newspapers and television channels. Except for Dabur, Tata, Bajaj and Videocon, all other top advertisers belong to the multinational category. Top brands that are being advertised in the media belong to these corporate. There has been a wave of foreign brands recently – all giving a big boost to the media as well as consumerism in such a way that as a country we cannot reverse the trend even if we want to.

Thirdly the advertising agency business in the country has been getting agency business in the country has been getting concentrated in fewer and fewer hands over the last few years. The top five advertising agencies, with majority holding abroad, account for well over half the advertising business in the country, and this trend has been on the increase. The entry of foreign advertising agencies has been going on alongside the entry of foreign brands and the increase in the share of foreign corporate in the total advertising in the country. In fact, lifting the limits of foreign capital in the advertising agency business has opened the floodgates. Now global conglomerates such as WPP, TWT, O&M, BBDO, DDB-Needham and JWT have gained majority control in Indian advertising and the bulk of the market share too. A little over half of all Indian advertising now is accounted for by agencies based abroad, whose majority control in India is with foreigners. In fact, among the top 20 agencies there may be just two without foreign partnership. Except for these, the others are answerable to either private groups based abroad or dollar-trading stock markets in London or New York.

Fourthly, market research is the basis for the proliferation of brands and consumerism, as well as for the preoccupation and priorities of the media, and the very scope and character of advertising. Until a few years ago we had six or seven market research agencies, mostly Indian-owned. Today the top seven or eight market research agencies, accounting for more than two-thirds the total number, have either been taken over by a foreign corporate or a foreign corporate has acquired a significant interest in them. In fact, with the recent mergers and acquisitions, a certain monopolistic trend is evident in this business, which has an annual turnover of over Rs. 350 crores.

More specifically, market research agencies conduct "readership" surveys and determine the "rating" of television viewership, and thereby directly influence advertising agencies as well as the media about their priorities and preoccupations. The point here is that the methodology being followed for readership surveys and TV ratings assessment is not without bias in favour of the sponsors and the subscribers. As the one who was involved in launching India-specific readership and rating studies 25 years ago, I feel guilty for what is happening today, particularly the way the findings of these surveys are being used both by newspapers and by TV channels. The "TRP trap", as I call the phenomenon, has larger and long-range implications for India than we seem to realise. The distortions are already evident in our media scene. This dilemma has been causing concern even in the United States at the highest levels of policy-making.

Fifth, with the media becoming complex and also specialised, two "new" mediating functionaries have emerged in the last two years, with serious consequences to the very nature and character of the Fourth Estate. Both these functionaries of media planning and public relations (PR) in a way erode the core prerogative of the media functionaries and their "editorial control". And the fact that both these functions have become corporatized, with foreign agencies in control, should cause some concern in the country before it is too late.

These days media planners are the ones involved in buying space and time wholesale for advertising and selling it on a retail basis on their terms. They are yet to expand nationally. Think of the implications, particularly because some of these corporate are controlled by foreign agencies and they have been in business in a big way trying to determine the terms of advertising in India. In a way, this amounts to undoing what Doordarshan initially did in term of providing a level playing opportunity to small and regional advertisers, by way of special concern for them so that they could compete with big corporate and in larger markets.

In the case of 'public relations', the functioning of these "experts" implies a certain undermining of or interference in the functioning, particularly of reporters and editors. For, the function of PR is to ensure coverage for a particular view point or otherwise. "Disinformation", which is being talked about recently, is a part of this new phenomenon. Today majority control of these PR corporate in India, some six or seven leading ones operating nationally, is with foreign agencies. In fact, some of these have entered India as a part of one or other advertising agency already having majority foreign equity. Most of these PR agencies cater to the interests of foreign corporate or their collaborators in India. Many Indian concerns, including some public utilities, now use the services of these PR agencies in order to make their presence felt in the media, as if it is a compulsion.

Giving out the findings of their analysis in this regard, P.N. Vasanti, Director of the Centre for Media Studies, New Delhi, said that "communication business has now moved into foreign control and this reflects on the scope of the content of newspapers, even more so in the case of television channels. Even Doordarshan's programming today is based on the guiding formula and criteria promoted by foreign-dominated agencies having their interest in big corporate".

Against this background, a debate on the entry of foreign capital into the print media is irrelevant and contradictory in view of what the government has already done by opening the floodgates to the electronic media.

Asian Age, September 12, 2001

The TV TR(A)P

By Dr N. Bhaskara Rao

The revelation made by CNBC on a possible "rating fudge" is significant since the priorities of Indian television are set by Television Rating Points (TRPs). "Stunned", "shocked" and "damaging" are some of the reactions of television channels. TRPs have always had a sacrosanct air about them a reason why the expose acquires the proportions of a "scam". But it is a wonder that despite the TRP-trap television in India has been under for some years, the intricacies were not brought out for public attention much earlier. Considering the consequences, the revelations should be viewed as a wakeup call for the industry.

This is not the first time that allegation of TRP manipulations have been made. This time, however, the vulnerability of the system being followed has been substantiated in such a way that larger public attention is guaranteed. TRPs were being taken for granted as a universal yardstick by media buyers, broadcasters, media, media users and by development planners at the highest levels in the country. Advertising agencies and advertisers have been doing their campaign planning and have been apportioning television spend amounting to some Rs. 4000 crores primarily based on such weekly ratings and, newspapers were busy hyping the "rating claims" by channels and content producers.

And yet there has hardly been any analysis in the media about what these TRPs are all about and at whose instance they are being compiled, the kind of methodology being used and with what reliability, and as to their very relevance in the context of the changing media scene and unique viewing situation in different households.

That these rating are only protections and for only a select few cities and based on a small sample of "representative" television households was not convincingly explained. The pattern of selecting television channels, viewing programmes, timings, etc, are measured with the help of a "people meter" installed in those selected few television households. The general impression often given is that these rating are national and represent all television owning households in the country. This is not fully correct. At best one would dare to say that they are indicative of the viewership in metro and major cities. Neither of the two rating services covers rural India. In fact, they cover only half of urban India. Starting with our metros about five year ago, the rating today cover 29 cities with some states or languages being covered by only one city.

The "peoples-meter" being used was developed for relatively homogenised societies and cultures such as Canada, the United State or South Africa and in fact, these meters were initially imported from these countries, mostly used ones. The buttons on such a meter in each sampled television household are expected to be pushed by each viewer as per his or her viewership. That is each viewer in the household is expected to be an "active" one to push the on-off button each time something on television is being watched.

The sample size of television household covered with the "people-meter" started with 400 and has now gone to 3454 in the case of TAM and 4405 in the case of INTAM. The sample size in case of some cities is around 120 and in the case of Mumbai it has been maximum--- today it is around 600. In these sampled panel households every member is expected to maintain strict confidentiality and use the on-off button of the meter without any inducement, or any pressure and each member is expected to use only the button assigned for her or him and do so each time of viewing during a 24-hour period and every day as long as the house is a member of the panel. Each such sampled household is expected to represent several thousands of television households or cable and satellite television households.

Any aberration in operating the on-off button, or any passivity in the process of any one member in the household will vitiate the projected ratings one way or other. If a few households in the "panel" of sample could be induced with incentives as is being done, the outcome is nothing but a manipulated one. The actual representative weight age of a household in a particular socio-economic category is another issue.

The spread of television to every nook and corner of the country and of regional language channels, has changed the scope and the extent of viewing. And yet the rating service is not extended to rural and small towns, despite 60 per cent of the television sets being there. Also, since nearly 60 per cent of television set are old black and white ones, the reliability or the "people-meter" is doubtful in capturing the viewership. Then, of course, the fact that the spread of channels is not uniform across different regions of the country all this brings out the inadequacy of the rating methodology presently being followed.

The 'people-meter' used was developed for relatively homogenised societies and cultures such as Canada, the United States or South Africa and in fact, these meters were initially imported from these countries, mostly used ones.

As a result channels having more viewership in rural India or among certain sections are disadvantaged in the ratings. That is, ratings based on urban viewership are deciding the programmes and programme schedules of television channels, including that of Doordarshan. The phenomenon of television being used as a decoration like a wallpaper in some households where on-off is not always related to actual viewing, is yet another issue.

The contents of "peoples-meters" are projected by desegregating the figures into several socio-economic-demographic classifications converted into a matrix of some 64 cells is another contentious issue in terms of accuracy levels. That is how competing channels often end up using these ratings to their own advantages picking up from out of these several variables. This is further complicated by the fact that there are two rating services in the market sometimes widely differing from each other although both use similar methodology and cater to same interests.

Both these services, TAM and INTAM, each charged anywhere between Rs 5,00,000 to Rs 50,000,00 as annual subscription (depending on the turnover of the subscriber), were driven by the interests of advertising from the very outset. Since advertising is primarily based on perpetuating and pampering consumerism, a rating service too caters to such interests. That is preferences and priorities of television channels and their programmes, their time schedules and formats, commercial tariff, etc., are all moderated by and based on these ratings. The two agencies are now engaged to merge rating services and perpetuate the TV anny of rating on Indian television. It is unfortunate that, not realising all this, Doordarshan got into this trap and lost its direction and priorities when it supported TRPs despite this authors efforts otherwise a few years ago.

Such ratings do serve in giving a "logic" for media planners to justify their large dispensations the total of which works out to some, Rs. 8000 crores annually. Hence the need for a certain transparency in the methodology and some independent monitoring and validation procedures. The routine replacement of a 10 per cent sample over a year is too little to ensure reliability of rating or to cope with passing and casualties in sampled television households week after week.

Since ratings are now "guaranteed" weeks before to lure advertising. It obviously implies that these ratings are a matter of survival for advertising agencies, content producers and to channels themselves. The kind of competition among them is such that it will intensify and lure them further. Obviously, organisations like the Indian Broadcasting Foundation (IBF) should take initiatives to bring in some discipline. Self-discipline any day is far better. The task of validation of ratings should not be left to users alone. In my opinion no one having any interest, direct or indirect, in advertising or is the media business be entrusted with such a task. They should however be associated with the exercise.

The architecture of "people-meter" and its practicality, once that scope is extended beyond cities is yet another issue that needs to be looked into. So that we have state of the art technology involving imaging and intelligent processing which allows the direct measurement of actual eye contact and reduces the chances of tampering.

Despite such meter based rating how much do we know about the "impact" of television on any part of the country or any section of society? For example on children? On a rough esterase the money involved between the two agencies, bring out TAM and INTAM is not less than Rs. 100 crores yearly. Recalling my own experience of bringing out the first ever National Readership Survey (NRS) reports and the fourth NRS, I know the kind of resistance and pressures coe faces in revealing facts not palatable to subscribers who are under constant threat from each other. What an effort for scratching the surface! Or shall we say for hijacking the priorities of idle vision and its very character?

CMS MEET
ON
TELEVISION VIEWERSHIP MEASUREMENT:
DILEMMA AND CHALLENGES
AT
INDIA INTERNATIONAL CENTRE
NEW DELHI
7 MARCH 2007
CMS MONOGRAPH ON DELIBERATORS

PREFACE OF P.N. VASANTI, DIRECTOR, CMS

It is no surprise that CMS meet on TV Viewership ratings has generated so much interest among so many different people. For it was the first time that a open forum had brought together rating agencies on one platform and also because the meet considered the concerns of general public rather than confining to the business interests of advertisers and TV channels. No one disagreed at the meet that rating of TV viewership should be preferably by independent agencies and that the process should be transparent and that since it is bound to have a say on the scope and schedules of contents of channels, the perspective of larger public cannot be ignored. That is now CMS initiative was appreciated and the meet felt that further initiatives are required by an independent group to examine issues to do with standards, regulation and technology of ratings. Because it felt that in the context of fast evolving technologies at the viewer end and emerge of a second rating agency, it is high time that a range of issues involved are further deliberated by those who have been seriously involved in shaping national policies as well as by those who are actually using the ratings.

It is astonishing that despite ratings have become the benchmark for priorities and pre-occupation of TV in India, no basic research of nay significance to validate or even assess and appraise the methodology, outcome and the role of ratings has been there. Perhaps because only a fraction of about two percent of revenues of TV, as spent in some countries whose viewership "market" is much smaller than India's, is being spent on research. This perhaps also explains why despite realization, even channels and advertisers, of limitations of "TRPs", they are contend with a service which hardly covers a quarter of population and even viewers and reflect any qualitative dimensions involved in viewing. It was also felt that the practice is without coming under any independent scrutiny at a time when every other such practice is being brought under a regulator and assuring transparency in the process.

It is heartening to see that both the old player (TAM) and the new player (aMap) shared their outlook and approach at this CMS Meet. aMap presentation included an overview of global scenario. It is obvious that the competition between the two is already causing a relook and revamp of the sample size and even the methodology. One issue which could not be deliberated at this meet however was to do with the "use of TRPs" by channels, sometimes denting the credibility of very rating. The other issue not discussed was about conflict of interest aspect of rating agencies.

In this monograph on the proceedings of day long CMS Meet we tried to present the discussion in verbatim to most extent. This publication is expected to help take the debate forward and also, in the process, sensitize more people about pros and cons of viewership rating operations and their implications to the kind of television channels and programme options we should have in the country. Your suggestions in this regard are welcome.

POSERS RAILED IN 2007 CMS ROUNDTABLE ON TRPS A DECADE AGO
ON 7TH MARCH 2007
SUMMING UP
SOME POSERS ABOUT TV VIEWERSHIP RATINGS

Relevance of Ratings:

- Why is so little spent for researching viewership patterns? (in more reliable, transparent, representative and specific to the unique socio-economic-media milieu of the country).
- Despite "viewership ratings" having devastating influence on the content priorities, schedules of channels, and even their very visibility, there is no independent assessment of the methodology being followed, its larger relevance and objectivity.
- The ratings have come into being to guide advertisers optimize their spend. Instead of limiting for such an internal exercise, the ratings have become the benchmark for setting the very priorities of TV and programmes of channels in the country- as if what interest viewers momentarily and what is in the interest of people is same!
- Measuring momentary viewing could be a first step for a more reliable understanding of viewership. But is mere "set-on or not" good enough for considering it as viewing? Is that always same as "preferred" or "liked" viewership?
- Such "instant viewership" could have limited relevance for a larger and reliable picture.
- It is said that these ratings have inhibited original Indian creative genius and plurality to come to fore, in different regions of the country as channels are made to "fall in line".

Reliability:

- The exercise should be transparent and representative such a way that channels of all size and regions and programmes, get fair change in the rating. Now, they are said to be advantageous more to big channels.
- The so-called "people meter" and its efficiency in capturing viewership of every one in a family, reliably and consistently has not been transparently validated. To what extent variation during "on and off" of buttons of "people meter" alter the reliability of ratings? What is the extent of compliance of "on" and "off" of specified button among different age groups and socio-economic households?
- Similarly, how relevant and reliable are the rating for news bulletins of general TV channels and "new channels" as compared to "entertainment" channels/Programmes?
- How can something become the benchmark or yardstick for the country without covering and reflecting rural India?
- By getting the cooperation of a few "active households" belonging to certain sections, can these ratings be generalized to large section of "passive viewers"?
- That is how there is a view that TRPs have hijacked TV in India with an altogether different priorities than what the potential of TV is for India.
- Some even say that TV channels are not able to get out of the trap of TRPs.

Usage:

- If rating for viewership is objective, how could there be conflicting claims by competitors sighting same source? Each channel is interpreting ratings as it suits and publicizing the way it suits even if it means mis-presenting.

The Agencies:

- The agency conducting ratings should be independent from the interests of advertisers and advertising agencies and individual channels.
- Who are these agencies conducting TRP? What is their origin and identity? As is said "where is their head and tail"? Is there any conflict of interests with their corporate?
- Should there be only one measurement or should there be competition between rating agencies – even it amounts more spending.
- Should there be independent regulation?
- The reliability of viewership ratings in the present system for small and regional language channels cannot be the same as for the big and national channels? As a result these channels, including Doordarshan channels, are being put to a disadvantage in the competitive scenario.
- Ratings are more an outcome and result of "aggressive marketing" by big channels and in fact, rating exercise and the outcome has become more part of "PR strategy" of channels.
- Why has regulatory authority not yet addressed the phenomena of TRPs? Should TRAI be looking into rating issues too? Even more important is viewing households should know more about these "ratings" practice so that they could more actively participate in the process.

References

The Past and the Present of Indian Television

1. *Jugalbandhi* is a term used in music performances where different sound instruments are played separately but to a tune, in order to echo a particular tune for particular sounds or and effect or outcome. The concept is used to express how different systems engaged in different functions operate in tandem or as if in coordination for certain results.
2. TRP (Television Rating Point) has come into circulation in India in the wake of AC Nielsen entry into India early 1990s. Nielsen was the premier television viewership rating agency in the USA where it had popularised the concept of TRP. Prior to this concept, the 'audit' and 'study' methods of surveys were used for indicating television viewership.
3. It was introduced for the first time on 15 September in Delhi, a decade after the British Broadcasting Corporation began regular service in 1936. With help from UNESCO, programmes about citizens' rights, civic duty, traffic sense and community health were broadcast twice a week for an hour a day.Two years later, these broadcasts were expanded to include educational programmes for school children.
4. N Bhaskara Rao, *Unleashing the Power of News Channels*, EMESCO, 2012.
5. N Bhaskara Rao, *Poll Surveys in Media*, National Book Trust, 2012.
6. FICCI (www.ficci.in) – KPMG (www.kpmg.com) Together they bring out an annual review of growth of media segments and the trends therein and project the volumes.
7. Centre for Media Studies media lab set up by CMS in 1991, in the wake of proliferation of round- the-clock news channels, monitors and analyses the contents of news channels. In the initial years, six news channels, three in Hindi and three in English, were monitored on a daily basis.

After a decade, once it was found that news bulletins of prime time (7-10 pm) were good enough to reliably reflect the news coverage, the media lab limited its monitoring to prime time over the years. Later, in 2004-5, CMS media lab started its operations in Hyderabad to monitor and analyse nine news channels which were at least two years old by then. Today the number of Telugu news channels are highest (over 30). next only to the number in Hindi in the country. Periodically, CMS has been conducting viewer studies in the specific context of an agenda-setting function, credibility and exposure to news media.

8. After a Special CBI court acquitted all 19 accused in the 2G spectrum allocation scam (said to be a scam of Rs 1.76 lakh crore, but CBI said it was just Rs 30,000 crore) in December 2017, the narrative has deteriorated further. As the 2019 general elections draw near, news channels are being accused of distinct political bias, of orchestrating a campaign against the incumbent government of 2012-14 and engineering a defeat by manufacturing a scam.

9. GNS Raghavan and N Bhaskara Rao, *Social Effects of Mass Media in India*, Gyan Publishing, 1996, New Delhi. Before becoming a professor in development communication at IIMC, Raghavan was a senior director in the Ministry of Information and Broadcasting. He was the author of important books including, *Understanding India*.

10 I understood much later why Vikram Sarabhai suggested that I should move to ORG. Three things made him take interest in me and suggested I should go to ORG Baroda. One was my rural roots and family background. Second my association with the first green revolution by way of promoting the until then unheard of nitrogen fertilisers (Urea), and my role in organising civil defence support campaign during the border conflict with China. Also because of the role I played in family planning communication. Third, my academic qualifications, a post-graduation in rural development and political science and a PhD in mass communication, it was a combination that Sarabhai felt was unusual then.

11. The entertainment - education model. In a nutshell it implies conveying something desirable purposely in a more easily acceptable context or format or frame. The process involves a learning or imparting behaviour or attitude change. Logics and linkages in behaviour and perceptions are often corrected, and it implies use of field research. Arvind Singhal and Everett M Roger's book, *Entertainment-Education and Communication Strategy for Social Change*, Lawrence Erlbaum, 1999 London.

12. Professor Wilbur Schramm was a pioneer in media research, communication scholar, and academic who had prompted communication studies in many US universities. He had advocated a distinct media model for developing countries. The model is based on the

belief that media can make a difference and hence should be concerned about socio-economic betterment of the country. He proposed that India go for cheaper or less expensive local options which is decentralised and participative of people. Schram met Prime Minister Indira Gandhi and argued in favour of radio and localised television as the better option for India's communication needs.

13. Everett M Rogers, *Diffusion of Innovation. Fifth Edition*, Free Press, 2003.

14. *Sesame Street* is the result of research by Children TV Workshop, USA in 1960-69. This serial was a first and based on extensive field research on cognitive learning. This serial was adopted in 17 global languages and broadcast in 53 countries. See Arvind Singhal & Everett M Rogers, *Entertainment – Education*, Lawrence Erlbaum Associates, 1999, pp 18-20.

15. *News Track* was the first weekly news video presented in anews bulletin style. Produced by and circulated to video cable operators and special subscribers by the India Today Group. (Year 1984-88) *News Track* was telecast on Star TV for one year (1998).

16. Birth of Commercial advertising in India starting with Doordarshan channels. Annual reports of the Ministry of Information & Broadcasting (www.mib.gov.in) and those of Doordarshan (www.ddindia.gov.in) and Prasar Bharati (www.prasarbharati.gov.in) gives the numbers year to year for channels.

17. Vicks was introduced in India in 1964, through a public limited company called Richardson Hindustan Limited (RHL). The parent company, Richardson Merrell, had established an office in India in 1951, but it was only with the institution of a public limited company with more than 10,000 Indian shareholders in 1964 that the brand gained operational freedom.
In the 1960s, RHL was one of many subsidiary companies selling Vicks across the world. Later, the company became a part of Proctor & Gamble.

18. The PIJ station in Kheda District (1978-80) was set up to demonstrate how locally relevant programmes could be broadcast. It was operated by ISRO with locally produced programmes and pre and post field research. The public were never told why the popular PIJ station was closed within two years. There was no opposition to any of its programmes.

19. A courtesy call on Indira Gandhi in 1976 by David Poindexter, director of the New York-based Population Communication, along with Migual Sabido of Mexico changed the future course of Indian television. At their recommendation, soap operas arrived but the idea of using them for social development and attitudinal change did not take root. With the interests of party-politics and advertising overtaking everything else in the

country, serious view of television as a tool and its potential did has not gained ground.

20. SS Gill (1985-88) was Secretary, Ministry of I and B, and it was his delegation that went to Mexico to discuss with Migual Sabido, the pioneer who popularised soap operas for entertainment - education in developing countries. Gill authored a book after retirement from service. Until his expose, it was not known that the Ministry and Prasar Bharati were at loggerheads on policy priorities. As a result, the Ministry never had decisive leadership, private channels expanded their networks and their active and assertive role. The best example of that was the way TRP came to be viewed as a benchmark for channels in the 190s despite the fact that Doordarshan channels, at that point in time, accounted for reaching much more than half of total television-accessed population.

21. A 1995 judgement of Supreme Court of India on broadcast rights remains a landmark. Although the judgement was in the context of cricket broadcast rights, because of its implications to the broadcast sector, it is referred to even after two decades as relevant and a missed opportunity for the nation. Despite government of the day accepting the judgment, it has not been adopted even after several promises on the floor of the Parliament.

22. Telecom Regulatory Authority of India (TRAI) was constituted in the year 1997 with responsibility to monitor the telecom sector.

    Broadcasting was not a part of TRAI mandate initially. But as the Ministry of I&B was not able to decide about a regulator for broadcasting as suggested by the Supreme Court judgement of 1995, and the issues to do with carriage aspect were becoming public, the Ministry entrusted the particular responsibility to TRAI in 2004.

    It was later in 2008, when the issue of ratings came under public criticism, the Ministry again passed on the responsibility to manage this controversy to TRAI. By then the Ministry had got the report of the Amit Mitra committee specially appointed following debates in the Parliament over viewership. It was based on that ad hoc assignment that TRAI came up with guidelines for viewership measurement and about the characteristics that the agency should have. TRAI's role specific to TV viewership ratings has become more important, with BARC becoming the agency to rate television viewership in place of TAM.

Content as Differentiator

1. For the last 25 years, CMS has organised a series of roundtable meets with stake holders on a range of issues in New Delhi and major centres

outside, starting with television and children in 1998 (21 November 1998). The participants included policy-makers, media members and activists.

The roundtable on the social effects of television was organised in six different locations outside New Delhi (1997-2000). The one on paradigm shift was organised in New Delhi and Hyderabad in 2004. Another one, exclusively with rating agencies, on television rating was held in New Delhi in 2007. At the end of most of these round tables, a monograph was brought out with list of participants in each case. While IK Gujaral inaugurated the CMS roundtable on children's TV, Former Chief Justice of India, Ranganath Misra was the keynote speaker. Monograph, 'Children and Television, a report, CMS, 21 November 1998'.

2. N Bhaskara Rao, Of content and control, *Frontline*, 14 September 2001 & Foreign Participation in Media, *Economic & Political Weekly (EPW)*, 12 January 2002.
3. TRAI. Telecom Regulatory Authority of India, guidelines 2013. www.trai.gov.in. Consultation paper No 7/2012.
4. CMS Media Lab has been tracking for more than 12 years regularly on a daily basis, 8 to 10 news channels in English and Hindi and 15 Channels in Telugu.
5. TRAI. Telecom Regulatory Authority of India, TRAI guidelines 2013. www.trai.gov.in. Consultation paper No 7/2012.
6. TRP by TAM India had become a criteria and the currency of the industry by 2000, that is in a matter of five years. This is evident from the content analysis of Telugu channels for the period. The three tables in this section sum up the trends for major Telugu channels for six years (2002-2007). The same trend was evident for Hindi and even English channels. CMS Media Lab, Hyderabad. Content analysis (2010) of Telugu news channels. www.tamindia.com
7. Shoma Munshi, *Prime time soap operas on Indian television*, Routledge, 2010, p75, 233-253 and 291.
8. Prosenjit Datta, *The Marketing White Book*, Section in 'Media and entertainment, the bright spots', *Business World*, 2014, p138-150.
9. Growth of Indian TV programme genre 2004-12. TAM (www.tamindia.com). Prosenjit Datta, *The Marketing White Book*, Section in, 'Media and entertainment, the bright spots', *Business World*, 2014.
10. Annual reports of Doordarshan (www.ddindia.gov.in).

11. Nalin Mehta, *Behind a Billion Screens: What Television Tells Us About Modern India*, Harper Collins, 2015. p 62-64.

12. The Chanda Committee (1968) was the earliest Parliamentary Committee on future course of broadcasting in India. AK Chanda was a member of Rajya Sabha (1967-74). Doordarshan was separated from AIR in 1976.

13. George Verghese was a sane voice of the decades (1967-2007), he was also press advisor to Prime Minister Indira Gandhi in different capacities. He had advocated for India a India- specific decentralised low-cost model of broadcasting. He was consistent that mass media should not lose track of their social responsibility and he reminded the nation of this, no matter which position he held. As Editor of the *Hindustan Times* (1982-86) his 'Chetera village (Haryana) endeavour' inspired many but unfortunately, once the new paradigm came into play, the model Verghese advocated was forgotten. He had authored a number of articles, policy papers and publications, including the UNESCO's MacBride Commission Report.

14. 1998-2000, article by N Bhaskara Rao, George Verghese and Dilip Padgaonkar in the edit page of *Hindustan Times*, 2005.

15. PC Joshi (1984-85), referred to in Sunetra Sen Narayan, *Globalisation and Television, a study of the Indian Experience*. Oxford, 2014. 1990-2010 (p. 200).

16. CMS PIL in Delhi High Court for taking up the Supreme Court recommendations and appoint an independent regulator before permitting direct to home television (DTH), without any India-specific conditions and obligations 1990-2010.

17. Kiran Karnik in 2001 in Sunetra Sen Narayan, *Globalisation and Television. A study of the Indian Experience 1990-2010,* Oxford University Press, 2014 Pages 121-123.

18. ibid.

19. ibid.

20. ibid.

21. Rama Bijapurkar, 'Consumer Syndrome', *The Week*; Anniversary Special, 28 December, 2008.

22. Sunetra Sen Narayan, *Globalisation and Television, a study of the Indian experience*, Oxford, 2014, pp 55-69.

23. Amit Mitra, now a Minister in the West Bengal government, was Secretary General of FICCI, when he was requested by the Ministry for a

report on future course on ratings of television viewership in the country. A general perception of the time was that he was asked not to antagonise the industry which had gained domination of television enterprise and for the Ministry to gain time.

24. Sunetra Sen Narayan, *Globalisation and Television, a study of the Indian Experience*, Oxford, 2014, p135 and 190.

    Shoma Munshi, *Prime Time Soap Operas on Indian Television*, Routledge, 2010, p.69.

25. *Live Mint,* 'The future of Doordarshan is on the block'. Html, (www.livemint.com)

26. 'Seeing is no longer believing' was a summative finding of CMS studies on credibility of news bulletins of twenty four-hour news channels. The content model was such that what one sees on television was not taken as real or true until confirmed by other sources. See for example *CMS monograph* of 2010, 'Why do TV news bulletins have to be always cluttered? Clutter of news', with foreword by Ramoji Rao, Chairman of ETV group.

27. G Parthasarathy, standing advisory committee to the Ministry of I&B (1980-03), felt that Doordarshan had lost its direction despite clear objectives laid down. A suggestion was that software priorities of television should be looked into and a direction be given. In response to this suggestion, the Ministry appointed the PC Joshi committee. This committee report on software was never put forth for public discourse and in fact, was not even taken up for a formal consideration by Doordarshan and the Ministry.

The Decade of Paradigm Shift

1. Rangnath Mishra, at CMS Round table in November 21, 1998, New Delhi, on children television, *CMS Monograph. p. 998.* Where he said that channels should be concerned that their broadcasting amounts to 'an undeclared war on an unprepared people'.

2. Dr N Bhaskara Rao & GNS Raghavan, *Social Effects of Mass Media in India*, Gyan, 1996. This book, just on the eve of proliferation of private and satellite channels, reminded people, the kind of implications content of television channels could have on children and women in particular, based on a sample survey and country wide seminars on the topic.

3. 1995 Supreme Court judgement continues to be viewed as a land mark despite successive Governments had ignored or were contended with TRAI. But development after 2010 brings out how ratings, for example, were being misused. The fifteen-year-old judgement reminds that an independent regulator is far more relevant today and it is high time that nation reminds itself that 'airways are public' and they are not merely for making money by the governments by public auctions but also transparent and accountable for larger public. Please see CMS Monograph, *Media Reforms. Freeing the Airwaves*, proceedings of national symposium, March 10, 1995.
4. Nalin Mehta, *Behind a Billion Screens: What Television Tells us About Modern India*, HarperCollins, 2015 P 78
5. Vinita Kohli Khandekar, *The Indian Media Business, 11th year of Publication*, Sage, New Delhi - 2015. P 140.
6. Niira Radia had convincingly conveyed in India that public relations executives influence policies, politics and decision makers by all kind of persuasions and lures. It was not known how until Radia's network and nature of 'deals' and the modus operandi of co-opting support of senior media personalities, including the industry leaders, Ministers and media leaders was exposed. She was a key person in what was known as the 2G scandal. She was heading a PR Agency known as Vaishnavi Corporate Communications. Web site www.vccpl.com
7. My visit to AC Nielsen New Jersey headquarters in US in 1986-87 as television was sweeping the country both in terms of spread and number of channels and range of programmes. As we at ORG at that time wanted to be familiar with the state of research in USA, I visited them at their New Jersey headquarter after prior appointment as President of ORG.
8. Based on an analysis of the trends in the contents of media particularly news media, and followed up with discussions with several decision makers in News channels, I came up with the observation that decisions as to what goes into news priorities, their positioning, focus and schedules are no longer decided by old gate keepers which meant subeditor, desk staff and editor but more by the rating agency, market researcher, media planner, and corporate public relations functionaries. These I called new gate keepers of India. See CMS monograph, *Media Scene as India Globalises*, CMS, September 2005.
9. ORG data base was based on my own notes as chief of ORG , which I compiled from out of store-audit and retail-audit reports brand wise off take in urban markets on a monthly basis and once a year in the case of

rural. Based on advertising monitoring reports of ORG for major mass media, the trends were analysed for some years until 2000.

10. Presenjit Datta, *Media and Entertainment: The Bright Spots* in *The Marketing White Book, Business World*, 2014. pp 150
11. Presenjit Datta, *The Marketing White Book, Business World*, 2014, P. 149. And Vanita Kohli-Khandekar, *The Indian Media Business*, Sage, 2013
12. Vanita Kohli-Khandekar, *The Indian Media Business*, Sage, 2013, pp 31-32, 140
13. CMS Media Lab and Vasanti Book, Percent of ad time channel wise in PN Vasanti & Prabhakar edited book, *TV News Channels in India*, Academic Foundation, 2016.
14. Dr N. Bhaskara Rao, *Mass Media and Marketing Communication perspectives into 2020*, 1995 CMS.
15. Sunetra Sen Narayan, *Globalisation and Television*, Oxford University Press, 2014 and Brand Equity, *Economic Times*, April 26, 2016
16. As Chief of World's largest communications services group WPP, Martin Sorrell has backed India's economic prospects. This group of WPP dominates the business of advertising agency, media planning, public relations firms, digital media, etc. for some years before 2000 and influenced government and private corporation policies to do with media, markets and consumer behaviours. It has stakes in consumer spending, advertising and sales promotions and consumption patterns. This group has more than half a dozen agencies in India and all of them promote viewership ratings and TRP culture. (www.wpp.com)
17. CV Srinivasan of Group M, *Business Standard*, February 14, 2014

The Origins of Ratings

1. 'Modi prisoner of his own image, practising TRP politics, Rahul Gandhi' by PTI in *The Economic Times*, December 3, 2016.
2. https://www.adgully.com/kantar-case-adjourned-by-delhi-hc-till-26th-august-58308.html
3. Amit Mitra (now Minister in West Bengal Govt.) was secretary general of Federation of Indian Chambers of Commerce (FICCI). At the height of criticism of TRPs and as the impression was that the industry was backing TRPs, the government thought it better to involve the apex body

of the industry in finding a way out of the dilemma. That was how Amit Mitra was roped in to come up with an option to TAM and what changes were required in TRP methodology, particularly sample size.

4. *Business Standard*, February 14, 2014,

5. Vidya Sahai, *Myths and Realities of TV ratings*, Press Institute of India, New Delhi, October-December 2005. pp. 34-37, *Vidura*-2005. This article was one of early critic of TRPs

6. DART, Doordarshan. Until 2000 Audience division of Doordarshan was engaged in analysing letters received from public voluntarily or on appeal and in conducting program specific field surveys. Major Doordarshan stations were having an audience research officer attached with one assistant doing some times panel studies among TV households at the instance of New Delhi. On mounting criticism of TRPs and on realising that Doordarshan was effected, Doordarshan took to DART (1992). Weekly viewership figures were put out every Friday based on personal interviews with a panel of TV households. As DART did not take competitive scenario in to account, nor reflected viewership to other TV networks, DART service could not be sustained, it was eased out just after two surveys, as if yielding to TAM's TRPs .

7. Rajini serial was a first serial featuring consumer activism in a real life scenario. It was a popular and well appreciated, produced by well-known eminent cinema director Basu Chatterji. I was with AG Krishna Murthy, CMD of Mudra Advertising, in Ahmedabad on one Sunday morning in mid-1986. Mudra was the sponsor for Rajini serial and known as sponsor of TV serials in the initial year. As we were watching Rajini at that time, he stated getting phone calls and after that he shared with me the kind of pressures to drop sponsoring Rajini and eventually he did succumb and it was not renewed and Rajini was dropped altogether. This incident was an early signal of what to follow with ratings becoming a formal mechanism.

8. Udai Shankar, *Business India* Interview, '*Vested interests delaying alternative rating agency*', *The Business Standard*, August 30, 2012.

9. I-map entered rating and positioned itself as a competitor to TAM's TRPs. To distinguish itself it talked initially and claimed itself as an on-line rating agency. It did so only symbolically by offering top line on selective basis. Ravindra Arora was finance director at Mudra advertising agency. He resigned and shifted to USA where he developed software for rating television viewership and packaged it as a regular service in the name of I -map.

10. How many meters were there until 2014? The number increased in

25 years from 500 to 9500 meters. And finally crossed 12,000 at the time BARC's take over (2014). BARC claimed 30,000 panel homes in 2018.

11. *Economic Times*, November 28, 2017
12. CMS round table in June 2004 in New Delhi and July 2004 in Hyderabad. See the monograph '*Opportunities and challenges. Indian media scene-recent shifts in paradigm of media operations*' CMS 2004. While the Union Minister for Information and Broadcasting, Jaipal Reddy was chief guest at New Delhi, Justice K. Jayachandra Reddy a former Judge of Supreme Court and sitting chair of Press Council of India chaired Hyderabad meet. Pradip Baijal, Chairman of TRAI was a key note speaker at New Delhi meet. Earlier in August 2000 Arun Jaitley was the chief guest at CMS roundtable.
13. Discussion with Mr Partho Dasgupta, CEO of BARC in Mumbai on November 17, 2017
14. 'Bar-o-Meter' is what BARC described the meters about half of meters it was using were same the earlier ones. TAM described the same as 'people meter'. (www.barcindia.co.in)
15. At the outset of meter based rating in 1993 I suggested that instead of a fixed panel sample, every round should have 10 to 15 percent new sample TV households and an analysis of two set of sample be compared and validated for reliability to replace panel members. When I reminded them of this suggestion in 2004 TAM claimed that it was doing that but there was no evidence of such practice. That there was no transparency in TAM's TRP operations was obvious.

Television Research: The Indian Case

1. Annenberg School of Communication in Philadelphia (another one is at Los Angles) is a Premier School and early one to initiate empirical studies on role and impact aspects of media particularly television channels from an inter disciplinary perspective. Dr George Gerbner, a pioneer on television and violence studies was the Director of Annenberg School of communication (1965-70). Time series studies in USA led by him on violence and children and coverage of television channels were taken note of by policy makers. I was invited to a conference (1967) in Philadelphia where initial findings were presented.

2. Wilbur Schramm, as earlier in chapter 1.
3. Arvind Singhal & Everett M. Rogers, '*Entertainment – Education*', Lawrence Erlbaum Associates, 1999.
4. NRS refer to chapter 1, NCAER (National Council of Applied Economic Research), www.ncaer.org , The National Family Health Survey is being conducted with the support of Ministry of Health and Family Welfare & USAID since 1992-93.
5. In conversation with Paritosh Joshi on November 17, 2017 in Mumbai, a member of BARC's three member committee on violations.
6. BARC has adopted 'impressions' as a way of indicating viewership. Earlier TAM used 'TRPs' for a decade and then shifted to TRT's and viewers. BARC did this change as semantics and also to enable it to 'show' higher numbers for viewership. For this 'impressing' in thousand could be differed by the times a viewer pushes the button on the meter and explain that as 'regional exposure'.
7. CEO of Prasar Bharati, KS Sarma who was earlier joint secretary in charge of AIR and Doordarshan in the Ministry, called senior functionaries of TAM from Singapore to discuss anomalies in TRPs. This he did not as a proactive initiative but because of mounting criticism and pressure from the Ministry for improving performance of Doordarshan. He also called me and Yogendra Yadav, known for poll surveys, as outside experts. The meeting requested TAM to present the reports and press releases that it did not represent rural India and certain states and reflect only a certain pre-selected metered TV households. Which TAM agreed to do henceforth but never did, not even once. Perhaps because Mr KS Sarma released the pending subscription to TAM without waiting for another couple of weeks!
8. CMS Vatavaran Festival was a specially designed, based on research insights of earlier 20 years, fest. The belief was that with research support complex problems involving behavioural change has to be taken up over a longer period and in a strategic way. This Vatavaran Festival is based on film and TV programmes on environment. Such complex issues are amenable for audio visual media.
9. Awards Narayan Rao, NDTV web site (www.ndtv.com), personal discussion and repeat news media reports. Also see CMS News TV Awards. See Dr N Bhaskara Rao, *Unleashing the Power of News Channels*, EMESCO, 2012. PP 128-137.

The Key Suspects

1. BARC press statement, November 23, 2016 (www.barcindia.co.in)
2. CMS round table on '*Television Viewership Measurement Dilemma and Challenges*', India International Centre, March 7, 2007, New Delhi.
3. Doordarshan Kendras (www.ddindia.gov.in)
4. Vidya Sahai, *Myths and Realities of TV ratings*, Press Institute of India, New Delhi October-December 2005. pp. 34-37, *Vidura*-2005. This article was one of early critic of TRPs
5. www.startv.com
6. TRAI guidelines left no option to IBF but to rally around an independent body, BARC, and be a sponsor. Thereby the claims of TAM that it was industry supported was put aside. For, TRAI had exposed conflict of interest aspect as well as representative character that TAM was claiming.
7. ECIL Meter... why TAM never tried to get the meters made in India over two decades and it rather preferred to import paying heavy import duty was a mystery. When it was known that ECIL could design and manufacture a meter more appropriate to Indian conditions and at a much cheaper cost. Instead, TAM appealed for exemption of customs duty.
8. BARC (www.barcindia.co.in)
9. With increase in public criticism that channels were not taking into account viewer's sentiments and as a pre-emotive initiative of government coming up with regulatory measures, channels took the initiative of welcoming complaints from viewers on any aspect of programmes. In response channels started calling for complaints at the instance of NBA or NBSA by putting up scrolls to this effect a few times every day.
10. IBF (www.ibfindia.com), TRAI (www.trai.gov.in)
11. Kantar CEO, Eric Salama was quoted in Indian Television.com's *New Millennium Special*, 31 January 2017.
12. See Udai Shankar, Chief of Star TV, *Vested interests delaying alternative rating agency*, *The Business Standard*, August 30, 2012.
13. *The Wire*, March 23, 2017
14. *Indian Express*, April 19, 2018
15. *Economic Times*, March 15, 2017.
16. *Mint*, November 25, 2016

17. *The Hoot*, December 15, 2016. (www.thehoot.org)

18. *Mint*, May 19, 2017

19. TRAI Guidelines P.15 Section 2:19 (www.trai.gov.in)

20. India Today, March 31, 1993

Fudging Ratings!

1. Estimate of metered household not reporting weekly; Personal discussions with LV Krishnan of TAM and Dasgupta of BARC.

2. Vidya Sahai, *Vidura*, October-December 2005. *Myths and Realities of TV ratings*, magazine of Press Institute of India, New Delhi. pp 34-37.

3. Nalin Mehta, *Behind a Billion Screens: What Television Tells Us About Modern India*, Harper Collins, 2015, P. 87

4. Opportunities & Challenges: Indian Media Scene 'Recent Shifts in Paradigm of Media Operations', CMS National Roundtable Discussions Friday, June 25, 2004, India International Centre, New Delhi and Saturday, July 31, 2004, at Centre for Economic and Social Studies, Hyderabad.

5. NDTV Case in New York Court as earlier (www.ndtv.com).

6. *Mint*, May 23, 2013. *Business India*, September 2, 2012. *The Hindu*, March 7, 2013. Dr N Bhaskara Rao, *Unleashing the Power of News Channels*, EMESCO, 2012, P 117-118.

7. *Mint* coverage on rating, November 25, 2016

8. PADMAJA SHAW reports, '*A TV grab from Telugu 360's sting operation*', Media Business, December 15, 2016. Padmaja Shaw's revelations on viewing was being manipulated in an organised way with specifics and quoting sources, was the first of such expose after BARC started ratings in 2014-15. It was to the credit of BARC that it took initiatives to cope with correctives. Padmaja Shaw was a professor at Osmania University Department of Communication, retired in 2016. http://www.thehoot.org/media-watch/media-business/telugu-360-sting-exposes-tv-ratings-manipulation-9850

9. BARC suspends rating of three TV channels, *Mint*, November 25, 2016 p. 112-118

10. TRAI meeting with senior advisor AK Gupta (He has become secretary

of TRAI since). To know whether TRAI was tracking implementation of its guidelines, I met in February 2017, the senior most functionary in TRAI who is incharge of television channels and viewership ratings. It was obvious that TRAI was geared up to do more of telecom than of electronic media. It operates more on request by the Govt. or on mounting public demand or on complaints by stakeholders. It is not so much a proactive body. It was on my bringing to his attention, for example, that he came to know of the kind of MOU signed between BARC and TAM.

11. Republic TV Channel toped charts on debut week itself, rivals exit measurement council by Harveen Ahluwalia, *Mint*, May 19, 2015.
12. NBA (www.nbanewdelhi.com)

Beyond a TRP Scenario

1. Justice AP Shah retired as Chief Justice of Delhi High Court. He had favoured monthly report of ratings instead of a weekly report.
2. *Indian Express*, April 15, 2018.
3. *Economic Times*, April 20, 2018
4. 'Indian Entertainment Biz Guide' of PICKLE, October 2017 featuring Viacom 18 Media The Great surge. (Distributed at CII meet).
5. 'Repositioning and way forward' in Dr N Bhaskara Rao, *Unleashing the Power of News Channels*, EMESCO, 2012. PP. 298-318
6. 14. Dr N Bhaskara Rao, *Mass Media and Marketing Communication perspectives into 2020*, 1995.
7. Supreme Court Judgement of 1995 as earlier.